RECKON

STRAYA

SANGER

MACCAS

WOOP WOOP

MOZZIE

MASTERING
AUSTRALIAN
SLANG & EXPRESSIONS

PASH

HARD YAKKA

LAPPY

FURPHY

RAPT

ELLA WALLABY

Contents

Welcome To The Land That Is Down Under!

G'day, mates! Welcome to *Mastering Australian Slang and Expressions: Your Essential Aussie Idioms Dictionary When You're Down Under.* This book is your golden ticket to chatting up the locals and understanding the quirky lingo that makes Australian English as colorful as a coral reef down at the Great Barrier. Ever been baffled by a convo down under, or do you just want to jazz up your vocab with some true blue Aussie slang? Either way, you're in for a ripper of a time!

From the sandy beaches of Sydney to the bustling streets of Melbourne, each Aussie phrase in this book is your insider guide to sounding like a local. I've packed this book with expressions I hear daily in Sydney, and I've laid them out alphabetically to make flipping through a breeze. There may be some you have heard or even use on the regular! But remember, Aussie slang can be as varied as our landscapes, so what you read here might just be the tip of the iceberg.

Why Aussie Slang, You Ask?

It's simple - Aussie slang is a doorway to the soul of Australia! It's all about the humour, the knack for not taking things too seriously, and a love for shortening just about any word. Whether you're planning a trip, love Australian films and shows, or just want to have a yarn with an Aussie mate, knowing the local slang will make your interactions richer and heaps more fun.

Inside This Book:

- **Key Aussie Slang and Idioms:** From "arvo" to "zhoosh," each term comes with a definition, a cheeky example, and a bit of backstory if it's particularly juicy.

- **Cultural Nuggets:** Get the scoop on when and how to use these expressions so you don't end up saying something's "as busy as a one-armed bricklayer in Baghdad" at a funeral.

- **Chuckler's Corner:** I've thrown in hilarious anecdotes to show how some of these phrases might play out in real life – because learning should be a laugh, right?

How to Dive In:
Jump into any section that tickles your fancy or start from A and work your way to Z. It's perfect for a read on the beach or a quick flick before a night out in Oz. And if you're heading over for a holiday or a study sesh, it's your perfect pre-trip read.

So, slap on your sunnies, grab a cold one, and let's get stuck into the vibrant world of Australian slang. By the end of this guide, not only will you be tossing around phrases like "no worries" and "she'll be right," but you'll also get the full picture that makes Aussie English as lively and welcoming as the people who speak it. Let's crack on, and trust me – fair dinkum, you're going to be speaking Aussie like you were born to it!

A

Ace

Definition: Ace is a term for excellent or very good. It is a positive affirmation of quality and satisfaction.

Example: After tasting the homemade pie at the local fair, Greg exclaimed, "That pie was ace!" The compliment made the baker's day, as she prided herself on her pie recipes. The term "ace" encapsulated the high standard and delight found in simple, well-made Australian treats.

Airs and Graces

Definition: Airs and graces refer to someone acting pretentiously or trying to appear more important or sophisticated than they are.

Example: Mrs. Jenkins put on airs and graces at the community meeting, flaunting her extensive travels and luxurious lifestyle. Her demeanor seemed out of place in the laid-back, egalitarian setting, where most people valued sincerity over pretension. The phrase humorously captured her exaggerated self-importance, contrasting with the Aussie value of keeping things real.

Akubra

Definition: Akubra is a brand of Australian bush hat, widely recognized as an iconic symbol of rural Australia and outdoor living.

Example: Wearing his Akubra, John felt a deep connection to the Australian bush heritage, its wide brim shielding him from the harsh sun. Tourists often purchased an Akubra as a cherished memento of their Australian adventures, embodying the rugged, adventurous spirit of the Outback. The Akubra was more than just a hat; it was a piece of Australian identity.

Anzac Biscuit

Definition: Anzac biscuits are sweet biscuits traditionally made from oats, flour, sugar, butter, golden syrup, baking soda, and boiling water, often including desiccated coconut. Named after the Australian and New Zealand Army Corps (ANZAC), they are historical treats from World War I.

Example: On ANZAC Day, Australians and New Zealanders bake Anzac biscuits to honor their soldiers' legacy. The biscuits symbolize the resilience and camaraderie of the ANZAC troops. Eating Anzac biscuits has become a way to remember and pay tribute to the sacrifices made by soldiers, bridging past and present through taste and tradition.

Amber Fluid/Amber Nectar

Definition: Amber fluid is a colloquial term for beer, reflecting Australians' fondness for this beverage and its integral role in social gatherings.

Example: At the local pub, the bartender asked, "What'll it be?" with a smile, the reply came, "A pint of your finest amber fluid, thanks!" This term speaks to the color of beer and its cherished place in Australian social life, where sharing a few pints is a common way to unwind and connect.

Aerial Ping-pong

Definition: Aerial ping-pong is a humorous or slightly derogatory term for Australian Rules Football. It highlights the sport's characteristic high kicks and catches (marks) that send the ball frequently into the air.

Example: At the family barbecue, Uncle Terry chuckled, "Are we watching the aerial ping pong match this weekend?" His playful jab at Australian Rules Football sparked laughter as everyone anticipated the game's dynamic action and aerial feats. Despite the teasing nickname, their excitement for the sport was undeniable, reflecting its deep-rooted place in Australian culture.

Ant's Pants

Definition: Ant's pants mean something is exceptionally good or impressive, akin to the American expression "bee's knees."

Example: Seeing the restored vintage car, Rob exclaimed, "Wow, that's the ant's pants!" The onlookers shared their admiration, agreeing on the vehicle's impeccable condition and style. The phrase "ant's pants" perfectly captured their collective awe and appreciation for something outstanding.

Argy-Bargy

Definition: Argy-bargy refers to a lively argument or dispute, often marked by a robust exchange of views or opinions.

Example: The town hall meeting descended into a bit of argy-bargy as residents debated the new development plan. Voices rose and fell in passionate discourse, with each side presenting its case fervently. The argy-bargy, while intense, demonstrated the community's deep engagement and concern for local issues.

Away With the Pixies

Definition: "Away with the pixies" means being lost in thought or daydreaming, not paying attention to the immediate surroundings.

Example: During the lecture, Lily seemed away with the pixies, her gaze distant and thoughts elsewhere. Her teacher's gentle reminder brought her back to reality, though her mind wandered to more fanciful places. The phrase "away with the pixies" charmingly captured her tendency to drift into a world of her imagination.

As Crook as Rookwood

Definition: "As crook as Rookwood" means being very sick or unwell, referencing Rookwood Cemetery in Sydney, one of the largest in the Southern Hemisphere.

Example: After eating something questionable, Jenna groaned, "I feel as crook as Rookwood." Her friends sympathized, knowing the phrase meant she was really unwell, and quickly fetched some remedies. The expression vividly conveyed her discomfort, linking illness with the finality and vastness of Rookwood.

Aussie Salute

Definition: The Aussie salute refers to the familiar gesture of swiping away flies with the hand, a familiar sight in rural and outback Australia.

Example: Chris frequently saluted the Aussie on the hiking trail, warding off the persistent flies buzzing around his head. This swatting motion, though simple, was an effective defense against the small but relentless pests. The Aussie salute, a blend of practicality and humor, epitomized the Australian approach to dealing with nature's minor annoyances.

Aussie Battler

Definition: An Aussie battler is an ordinary Australian who perseveres through hardships with resilience and determination, embodying the national spirit of hard work and fairness.

Example: Linda, a single mother working two jobs, was known as a true Aussie battler in her community. Despite the challenges, she maintained a positive outlook, earning the respect and admiration of her neighbors. Her story was a testament to the Aussie battler spirit, showcasing the strength and perseverance admired in Australian culture.

Avo

Definition: "Avo" is an Australian slang for "avocado." It's part of the Australian penchant for abbreviating words in everyday speech, making them more casual and friendlier. This abbreviation reflects the popularity of the fruit in various dishes, particularly in brunch items like avocado toast.

Example: "Could you add extra avo on that toast?" Claire asked the waiter, eager to enjoy a hearty serving of her favorite creamy, green fruit with her morning meal. The cafe was known for its lavish spreads of avo toast, which drew in a crowd eager for a delicious, nutritious start to their day.

B

Bag Out

Definition: "To bag out" means to harshly criticize someone or something, often to express strong disapproval or disappointment.

Example: After the football match, fans began to criticize the referee for what they saw as unfair decisions. The heated discussions continued long after the game, with supporters venting their frustrations over what they perceived as poor officiating.

Banana Bender

Definition: Banana bender is a playful nickname for a person from Queensland, referring to the state's tropical climate and association with banana growing.

Example: At the interstate rugby match, the commentators joked about the number of banana benders in the Queensland team. The nickname, used affectionately, showcased the regional pride and friendly rivalries that enrich Australian sporting culture.

Banged-up

Definition: Banged up means to be injured or in a bad state, often referring to physical damage or ill health.

Example: After the rough rugby match, Dave was all banged up, with bruises and a sprained ankle, a testament to the game's intensity. His teammates ribbed him good-naturedly, his battered condition a badge of honor in the harsh world of sports.

Bathers

Definition: Bathers refer to a swimsuit or swimwear, the preferred term in many parts of Australia.

Example: On a hot summer day, everyone at the beach was in their bathers, enjoying the sun, sand, and waves. The colorful array of bathers, from bikinis to board shorts, painted a vibrant picture of Australian beach culture..

Barbie

Definition: Barbie is an Australian term for barbecue, a social event where food, especially meat, is cooked outdoors on a grill or open fire.

Example: The Smith family hosted a Barbie every Australia Day, inviting neighbors and friends for a day of grilling, laughter, and community.

Beaut, Beauty

Definition: Beaut or beauty is an expression used to describe something or someone excellent, fantastic, or of high quality.

Example: When Mark unveiled his restored vintage car, his mates exclaimed, "That's a real beaut!" With its gleaming paint and polished chrome, the car stood as a testament to his hard work and was considered a beauty by all who saw it.

Belt up

Definition: "Belt up" can either mean fastening the seat belt in a vehicle or, colloquially, telling someone to stop talking or complaining.

Example: As they hit the road, Mike told his chatty brother to belt up for safety and to get some peace and quiet. The dual meaning brought a moment of humor to their journey, highlighting Australian communication's practical and playful sides.

Best Thing Since Sliced Bread

Definition: This phrase describes a good invention or innovation, something highly valued and appreciated, implying it's a significant improvement over what existed before.

Example: When the new smartphone model was released, tech enthusiasts called it the best thing since sliced bread. Its advanced features and sleek design set a new standard, making it a highly praised addition to the tech world.

Buggered

Definition: Buggered means fatigued, exhausted, or sometimes broken, often used to describe physical or mental weariness.

Example: After the marathon, Lisa collapsed on the grass, and told her friend who ran with her, "I'm buggered."

Billabong

Definition: A billabong is a river branch forming a backwater or stagnant pool of water flowing from the mainstream during a flood.

Example: On their hike through the Outback, the group discovered a serene billabong, teeming with birdlife and native plants. This tranquil spot, hidden from the main river, offered a peaceful escape and a perfect example of Australia's unique natural beauty.

Bickie

Definition: "Bickie" is a typical Australian term for biscuit, showcasing the Australian tendency to abbreviate words.

Example: At the afternoon tea, guests were offered a selection of bickies to accompany their drinks. From chocolate chip to Anzac, each bickie was a delight, turning the simple snack into a beloved treat.

Billy

Definition: A billy is a tin or enamel pot used for boiling water, especially while camping or outdoors in Australia.

Example: Around the campfire, the travelers used a billy to boil water for their tea, embracing the traditional Australian way of making a bush brew. The ritual of using the billy connected them to generations of Aussies who had traversed and camped in the vast Australian landscape.

Bizzo

Definition: "Bizzo" is a slang term for business, often used in the phrase "mind your bizzo," which means to mind your own business or affairs.

Example: When asked about his weekend plans, Tom retorted, "Just mind your bizzo," wanting to keep his personal life private. The term "bizzo" encapsulated his desire for discretion, a common sentiment in maintaining personal boundaries.

Bloke

Definition: "Bloke" is a common Australian term for a man, often used informally to refer to an average, everyday guy.

Example: Dave is a great bloke, always ready to lend a hand or crack a joke.

Blimey

Definition: "Blimey" is an exclamation of surprise or astonishment, often used to express shock or amazement.

Example: "Blimey, did you see that kangaroo jump right over the fence?" exclaimed Pete, his eyes wide with disbelief. Australian wildlife's spontaneous nature often leads to "blimey" moments for locals and visitors.

Blind

Definition: In Australian slang, "blind" means extremely drunk, often used to describe someone who has consumed a significant amount of alcohol.

Example: For example, after the rugby final, the celebrations went on late into the night, and some fans ended up getting absolutely blind. The term "blind" captures the intensity of their festivities and the level of overindulgence.

Bugger All

Definition: Bugger all means very little or nothing at all, used to express a lack of quantity or significance.

Example: After hours of fishing, Mike sighed, "We've caught bugger all today." This expression captured the frustration and disappointment of returning empty-handed.

Bring a Plate

Definition: "Bring a plate" is an invitation to bring a dish of food to share at a social gathering, emphasizing communal eating and sharing.

Example: When invited to the neighborhood block party, guests were asked to bring a plate. This tradition of sharing food fostered a sense of community and connection, as each person contributed to the feast, showcasing a variety of homemade dishes.

Bull Bar

Definition: A bull bar is a strong metal grille bar fixed to the front of a vehicle, designed to protect it from collisions, particularly with wildlife in rural areas.

Example: In the Outback, it was common to see vehicles equipped with bull bars, a necessary precaution against unexpected encounters with kangaroos and other wildlife on remote roads.

Bush

Definition: The bush refers to rural, undeveloped areas of Australia, akin to the wilderness or natural countryside, characterized by native vegetation and wildlife.

Example: John loved escaping to the bush on weekends, finding solace in its tranquil and untouched landscapes, a stark contrast to the city's hustle and bustle.

Bush Bash

Definition: Bush bash can mean driving off the main roads through the bush or refer to a rough, informal party held in a rural setting.

Example: The adventurous group decided on a bush bash, taking their 4WD off-road to explore the hidden beauty of the bush. In another context, the local youth held a bush bash, a spontaneous party under the stars filled with music and laughter.

Busy as a Bee

Definition: Busy as a bee means being very busy or active, reflecting bees' constant movement and industrious nature.

Example: In the lead-up to the festival, the organizers were as busy as bees, coordinating every detail to ensure the event's success. Their energy and dedication mirrored the tireless work of bees in a hive.

Blue

Definition: In Australian slang, a "blue" refers to a fight or argument, often a heated or physical dispute.

Example: The disagreement at the pub escalated into a bit of a blue, drawing the attention of everyone present. While "blues" are generally frowned upon, they are sometimes seen as a passionate, if not misguided, expression of strong opinions.

Boot

Definition: In Australian English, the term "boot" refers to the trunk of a car. The compartment at the vehicle's rear is used for storing items such as luggage, shopping bags, or equipment.

Example: Before heading out on their weekend road trip, they packed the car's boot with all their camping gear, ensuring everything from the tent to the cooler was securely stowed. The efficient packing allowed them to maximize space, providing a comfortable and organized journey.

Blow the Froth Off a Few

Definition: "Blow the froth off a few" is an Australian phrase that describes going out to drink beer, often in a casual and social setting. The expression humorously refers to sipping the frothy top-off cold beers enjoyed among friends.

Example: Mike suggested they blow the froth off a few after a long week of work at their favorite local pub. The group shared laughs and stories over their beers, gathered around a table.

Bob's your Uncle

Definition: "Bob's your uncle" is a phrase used to indicate that a task has been completed or a situation resolved, implying that everything is in order.

Example: "Just turn the knob and push the button, and Bob's your uncle, the machine starts right up," explained the mechanic, demonstrating the simplicity of the operation. The phrase conveys a sense of ease and finality, assuring that all is well and straightforward.

Bogan

Definition: A bogan refers to an individual perceived as unsophisticated or of lower social status, often characterized by their lack of cultural tastes and coarse behavior.

Example: At the concert, a few bogans in the crowd were getting rowdy, their loud shouts and rough manners standing out. Despite the negative stereotype, some embraced the bogan identity with a sense of humor and pride, challenging the social stigma associated with the term.

Boomer

Definition: A boomer is a giant male kangaroo known for its size and strength. The term can also refer to something very large or significant in size.

Example: While hiking in the national park, they spotted a boomer watching them cautiously from a distance. Its impressive size and muscular build were a magnificent sight, epitomizing the wild and untamed essence of the Australian bush.

Bush Telly

Definition: Bush telly refers humorously to a campfire, mainly when used as the main focus of entertainment and gathering in the absence of technology.

Example: At night, the campers sat around the bush telly, sharing stories and watching the flames dance, the campfire serving as their screen and the stars their backdrop in the great outdoors.

Bottl-O

Definition: Bottl-O is a colloquial term for a bottle shop or liquor store where alcoholic beverages are sold.

Example: On his way to the party, Dave stopped by the bottle-o to pick up a case of beer. The local bottl-O was a convenient stop for those looking to purchase alcohol for various occasions, from casual get-togethers to formal celebrations.

Bounce

Definition: To bounce means to leave or go away from a place, often used informally to indicate departure.

Example: After a quick chat, Jake said, "I've got to bounce, mate. Catch you later!" The term 'bounce' added a casual and friendly tone to his farewell, reflecting the laid-back nature of Australian social interactions.

Brekkie

Definition: Brekkie is a colloquial term for breakfast, often used in casual conversation.

Example: "Let's grab some brekkie before we start the day," suggested Tom, eager to start the morning with a good meal. The term' brekkie' reflected Australians' informal and friendly approach towards the day's first meal.

Brickie

Definition: A brickie is a slang term for a bricklayer who lays bricks to construct or repair walls and other structures.

Example: Working under the hot sun, the bricklayer skillfully laid each brick, demonstrating expertise through the speed and precision of his work. The bricklayer's role in building and construction is integral, highlighting the skilled labor that shapes the country's infrastructure.

Budgie Smugglers

Definition: "Budgie smugglers" is an amusing Australian term for men's tight-fitting swimwear, similar to Speedos. The phrase humorously implies that the swimwear is so tight it resembles a small cage containing budgerigars (budgies), a popular type of small Australian parrot.

Example: At the beach, everyone chuckled as Dave strutted around in his budgie smugglers, drawing attention with his bold choice of swimwear. The term perfectly captured the snug fit and daring nature of his outfit, much to the amusement of his friends.

C

Chips

Definition: In Australian English, "chips" can mean two different types of food depending on the context. It can refer to the thin, crispy potato snacks known in the United States as "potato chips" or the thicker, fried potato cuts known as "French fries" in the U.S.

Example: At the beachside café, they ordered a large serving of hot chips, which arrived golden and steaming, accompanied by various dipping sauces.

Call it a Day

Definition: "Call it a day" means to stop working on something for the rest of the day, often after completing a significant amount of work or reaching a natural stopping point.

Example: After several hours of intense gardening, Marie wiped her brow and decided to call it a day, feeling satisfied with her progress and knowing the rest could wait until tomorrow.

Carry on Like a Pork Chop

Definition: To "carry on like a pork chop" means to behave in a foolish, dramatic, or exaggerated, often attracting unnecessary attention.

Example: During the meeting, Pete carried on like a pork chop over a minor issue, causing eye rolls among his colleagues. His over-the-top reaction was seen as unnecessary and disruptive, much like the idiom suggests.

Chuck a Sickie

Definition: To "chuck a sickie" is to take a day off work pretending to be sick, often when an employee wants a break but is not ill.

Example: Feeling burned out, Mark decided to take a sick day, spending the day at the beach to recharge instead of going to the office. The phrase reflects a common practice in workplace culture: balancing honesty and self-care.

Chock-a-Block

Definition: "Chock-a-block" means whole, crowded, or packed, often used to describe a place or container with no remaining space.

Example: The tiny café was chock-a-block with customers eager to try the famous brunch menu, illustrating its popularity and the tight squeeze inside.

Come Good

Definition: "Come good" means to turn out well in the end, especially after difficulty or uncertainty.

Example: Despite the project's shaky start and numerous challenges, it eventually came good, surpassing everyone's expectations and achieving great success. The term reflects the optimism and hope that, despite early problems, things can improve and yield positive results.

Couldn't Run a Chook Raffle

Definition: Saying someone "couldn't run a chook raffle" implies they are incompetent or unable to organize a simple event or task, with a chook raffle being a relatively straightforward fundraising activity.

Example: When the office party turned chaotic, someone remarked that the organizer couldn't run a chook raffle, highlighting the disorganization and lack of planning evident in the event's execution.

Crikey

Definition: Crikey is an exclamation of surprise, astonishment, or disbelief, often used to react to something unexpected or impressive.

Example: "Crikey, look at the size of that snake!" exclaimed Tom, his eyes widening in amazement at the creature crossing their path. The word crikey captured his spontaneous reaction to the unexpected encounter in the wild.

Crook

Definition: Crook can mean either sick or poorly made, and it also describes something dishonest or illegal. The context usually clarifies the intended meaning.

Example: Feeling crook after eating spoiled food, Jenna had to miss work. In a different context, a local scandal revealed a crook deal that shocked the community. The dual use of crook in Australian English illustrates the word's flexibility and range of application.

Cranky

Definition: Cranky means being bad-tempered or angry, often used to describe someone who is easily irritated or in a foul mood.

Example: After a sleepless night, Sarah felt particularly cranky, snapping at minor annoyances she would typically ignore. Her crankiness was evident to everyone, making them tread carefully around her until her mood improved.

Cuppa

Definition: Cuppa is a commonly used term for a cup of tea or coffee, often signifying a break or a moment of relaxation.

Example: "Let's have a quick cuppa," suggested Ann, signaling a pause in their busy day for a soothing drink. The invitation for a cuppa represented a universal gesture of hospitality and comfort in Australian culture.

Crack the Shits

Definition: "Crack the shits" is a crude but commonly used Australian expression for becoming extremely angry or upset. It vividly describes someone's frustration boiling over into intense, visible anger.

Example: After seeing the mess in the living room for the third time that week, Sam cracked the shits, yelling for everyone to start cleaning up. His patience had worn thin, and his sudden outburst left no doubts about his level of frustration.

Come the Raw Prawn

Definition: "Come the raw prawn" is an Australian slang term used to accuse someone of attempting to deceive or fool others. The phrase suggests presenting something false or unconvincing, akin to offering an uncooked prawn as something appealing.

Example: When Gary tried to convince everyone that he had won the lottery, his sister accused him of coming to the raw prawn, knowing he was just spinning a tale. His unconvincing details and mischievous grin made it clear he was just trying to pull one over on them.

Chuck a U-ey

Definition: "Chuck a U-ey" is an Australian colloquial term used to describe making a U-turn in a vehicle. The phrase is a casual, direct way to instruct someone to turn the car around and head in the opposite direction.

Example: Lisa told Jake to chuck a U-ey at the next intersection, realizing they had missed the park entrance. With a glance over his shoulder and a turn of the steering wheel, they soon headed back the way they came, making the maneuver effortlessly.

D

Doover

Definition: In Australian English, "doover" is a casual term similar to "thingamajig," which refers to an object whose specific name is temporarily forgotten or unknown.

Example: As she tried to assemble her new furniture, she rummaged through the toolbox, muttering, "Where's that doover for tightening these screws?" Unable to recall the exact name, she used the trusty doover to get the job done.

Duvet

Definition: A duvet, often interchangeable with "quilt" in Australia, is a type of bedding consisting of a soft flat bag filled with down, feathers, wool, or synthetic alternatives and often encased in a removable cover.

Example: On a chilly winter night, she snuggled under her warm duvet, the soft filling providing perfect insulation against the cold. The cozy comfort of the duvet made her feel instantly relaxed and ready for a good night's sleep.

Comforter

Definition: Known as a quilt or duvet in some regions, including Australia, a comforter is a thick, fluffy bedding item typically used for warmth. It is made from two layers of fabric filled with insulating materials like down or synthetic fibers.

Example: She decorated her bedroom with a vibrant new comforter, adding a splash of color and a layer of warmth to her bed. The plush comforter made her room feel more inviting and luxurious, perfect for cozying up on lazy weekends.

Daks

Definition: Daks is a slang term for trousers or pants.

Example: "I've got to buy some new daks for the wedding," said Liam, realizing that his old ones no longer fit. The term 'daks' is commonly used in everyday conversation, reflecting the casual style of Australian speech.

Damper

Definition: Damper is a traditional Australian bread made from flour and water and usually cooked in the ashes of a campfire.

Example: On their camping trip, they made damper, a rustic and satisfying experience of preparing and eating this iconic Australian bush tucker. Cooking damper by the fire connected them to a longstanding tradition, highlighting a simple yet fundamental aspect of Australian outdoor life.

Deadset

Definition: Deadset means certain or severe about something; it can also mean genuine or authentic.

Example: "I'm deadset on going to Uluru this year," declared Jenna, her determination clear. Her deadset attitude reflected her strong commitment and earnestness about the trip.

Devo

Definition: Devo is a shortened form of 'devastated,' used to express extreme upset or disappointment.

Example: When the concert was canceled, fans were devo, their hopes dashed after months of anticipation. The slang 'devo' succinctly conveyed the depth of their disappointment.

Digger

Definition: Digger is a colloquial term for an Australian soldier, especially those who served in World War I. However, it has come to represent Australian soldiers in general.

Example: The memorial service paid tribute to the diggers who had served the country; their bravery and sacrifice were honored in speeches and ceremonies that highlighted the enduring legacy of the diggers in Australian military history.

Dob in

Definition: To dob in means to inform on someone, typically in a negative sense, akin to snitching or telling on someone.

Example: When the school prank went too far, someone dobbed in the culprits to the teacher. Dabbling is often viewed with mixed feelings, as it involves revealing information that could get others into trouble.

Dipstick

Definition: Dipstick is a slang term for someone seen as foolish or inept.

Example: "Don't be such a dipstick," laughed Sarah as her brother clumsily attempted to set up the tent. His lack of skill turned the task into a comedy of errors. The word 'dipstick' added a playful, teasing element to the interaction.

Dodgy

Definition: Dodgy means something that is suspicious, unreliable, or of poor quality, often implying a lack of trustworthiness or a risk of malfunction.

Example: The car dealer offered a used vehicle at a surprisingly low price, but it looked a bit dodgy, with its inconsistent paintwork and rattling engine. Buyers learned to be wary of dodgy deals that seemed too good to be true.

Dog's Breakfast

Definition: A dog's breakfast is extremely messy or disorganized, often resembling the scattered appearance of a dog's meal.

Example: The project report was a dog's breakfast, with pages out of order and numerous errors, leading to a complete overhaul. The term captured the document's chaotic state, necessitating a more structured and careful approach.

Dunny

Definition: In Australian English, Dunny is a colloquial term for a toilet or outhouse, especially an outdoor one.

Example: At the old farmhouse, the outside dunny was quirky, reminding visitors of bygone days before indoor plumbing became common. Dunny is often used affectionately or humorously when referring to rustic toilet facilities.

Drongo

Definition: Drongo is an Australian slang term for someone foolish, incompetent, or lacking in common sense, often used in a playful or derogatory manner.

Example: "Don't be such a drongo, mate," laughed the group, as Jeff forgot the most basic camping essentials on their weekend trip. The term drongo humorously highlighted his oversight and added a light-hearted ribbing to the situation.

Dog's eye

Definition: Dog's eye is rhyming slang for a meat pie, a popular snack in Australia, often consumed at sporting events or as a quick meal.

Example: At the footy match, fans queued up for a dog's eye and sauce, the classic Australian game-day fare.

Down Under

Definition: Down Under is a colloquial term for Australia. It refers to its location in the southern hemisphere, "below" many other countries globally.

Example: Many tourists dream of a trip Down Under, attracted by images of Australia's vast landscapes, unique wildlife, and vibrant cities. Down Under evokes a sense of adventure and the allure of exploring a distant and exotic land.

Durries

Definition: Durries is Australian slang for cigarettes, a casual term often used in informal settings.

Example: "Got any durries on ya?" asked the man outside the pub, looking to borrow a smoke from a fellow patron. The use of durries in this context reflects the laid-back nature of Australian social interactions, especially among smokers.

E

Earbash

Definition: To earbash means to talk incessantly or to nag someone, often in an overwhelming or annoying way.

Example: Gary earbashed his friend about the importance of saving money, going on so long that his friend jokingly begged for mercy. The term perfectly captures the experience of being on the receiving end of a relentless, forceful conversation.

Easy as

Definition: "Easy as" is a phrase that describes something very easy or straightforward, often left incomplete, implying "easy as pie" or a similar expression.

Example: Completing the puzzle in record time, Jess smiled and said, "Easy as," showing her confidence and skill. The phrase emphasizes the simplicity and lack of difficulty in accomplishing the task.

Egg Beater

Definition: Eggbeater is slang for a helicopter, humorously alluding to the rotating blades resembling the beaters of a kitchen appliance.

Example: The children were fascinated by its spinning rotors and loud noise as they watched the egg beater landing in the field. The term playfully describes the helicopter's appearance and function, bringing a smile to their faces.

Elbow Grease

Definition: Elbow grease refers to hard physical effort, particularly in cleaning or manual labor, suggesting that the task requires vigorous use of one's arms or elbows.

Example: The old table looked brand new after some serious elbow grease was applied, scrubbing away years of dirt and grime. The term conveys the intense effort and exertion needed to achieve a sparkling clean result.

Esky

Definition: An Esky is a brand name that has become a generic term for a portable cooler used to keep drinks or food cold, essential for picnics, barbecues, or outdoor events in Australia.

Example: By packing the Esky with ice and beverages, they prepared for the beach picnic, ensuring they'd have cold drinks on a hot summer day. The Esky is synonymous with outdoor leisure in Australia.

Every Man and His Dog

Definition: "Every man and his dog" is an expression used to indicate many people, often humorously implying that a place is highly crowded.

Example: At the town fair, it seemed like every man and his dog had turned up, making it a bustling, lively event filled with community spirit.

Even Stevens

Definition: "Even Stevens" describes a situation where two sides are equal, fair, or balanced, with no apparent advantage for either side.

Example: The game finished even with Stevens, with both teams performing equally well and ending in a draw. All involved saw this result as fair and satisfactory.

Everything but the Kitchen Sink

Definition: This phrase includes almost everything imaginable, whether necessary or not, and is often used to describe overpacking or overpreparation.

Example: For the weekend camping trip, they packed everything but the kitchen sink, bringing far more than they needed, just to be on the safe side.

End of the Road

Definition: "End of the road" is an idiom used to signify the conclusion or final point of a journey, whether physical or metaphorical.

Example: After months of trying to save the failing project, the team acknowledged it was the end of the road; no more options were left to explore. Accepting this, they began to focus their energies on new endeavors, recognizing that some paths inevitably end!

Excuse me for Living

Definition: "Excuse me for Living" is a sarcastic response to someone's criticism or rebuke. It is used to express indignation or disbelief at the harshness or unfairness of the comment.

Example: I remember one time I made a minor mistake and someone criticized me for it. I exclaimed, "Excuse me for a living!" because I was so frustrated with the overreaction to such a small oversee on my part.

Excuse my French

Definition: "Excuse my French" is a phrase used to apologize for swearing or using profanity. In Australian usage, it's often used after someone has said something rude, cheekily pretending that the offensive words are part of a foreign language.

Example: After dropping the plate, Claire exclaimed a curse and quickly added, "Excuse my French!" Her light-hearted apology drew a laugh from her friends, smoothing over the momentary slip with a touch of humor characteristic of this idiom.

F

Fair Dinkum

Definition: Fair dinkum means genuine, authentic, or honest, often used to express authenticity, truth, or sincerity in Australian English.

Example: When he shared his outback adventure stories, everyone knew he was fair dinkum. His detailed accounts and genuine demeanor left no doubt about his experiences.

Flanno

Definition: Flanno refers to a flannel shirt, a wardrobe staple of rural workers and often associated with the stereotypical Australian 'bogan.'

Example: Wearing his favorite flanno, Dave attended the local footy game, embodying the laid-back, no-fuss style celebrated in Australian culture.

Furphy

Definition: A furphy is a rumor or untrue story, often an exaggerated or tall tale, originating from water carts made by Furphy & Sons that bore the company name and became gathering points for exchanging gossip.

Example: The story of the haunted mansion on the hill turned out to be a furphy, delighting locals with its mysterious origins but lacking objective evidence.

Feral

Definition: Feral describes something wild, untamed, or uncontrolled. It is often used to depict a person's wild behavior or unkempt appearance.

Example: After weeks in the wilderness without proper amenities, he looked somewhat feral, his hair unkempt and his demeanor wild, embodying the ruggedness of his adventure.

Fairy Bread

Definition: Fairy bread is an Australian treat made by sprinkling hundreds and thousands (colorful nonpareils) on buttered white bread. This simple, sweet snack is a staple at children's birthday parties.

Example: At Lucas's fifth birthday, the fairy bread was the biggest hit. Children eagerly grabbed the colorful, sugary pieces, embodying the joy and whimsy of the celebration.

Fairy Floss

Definition: Fairy floss is the Australian term for cotton candy, a sugary treat spun from colored sugar popular at fairs and carnivals.

Example: At the country fair, children clustered around the stall selling fairy floss, eager to get their hands on the fluffy, sweet confection that has become synonymous with outdoor festivities.

Fisho

Definition: Fisho can refer to a fisherman or a person selling fish, often associated with the fishing industry or local fish markets.

Example: Every morning, the local fisho set up his stall at the market, offering the freshest catch to customers who trusted his expertise and loved his seafood.

Fancy That

Definition: "Fancy that" is an expression used in Australia to convey surprise or amazement about something. It indicates that something is unexpected or particularly noteworthy, and it is often used in response to hearing interesting or surprising news.

Example: When Tom mentioned that he had bumped into their old high school teacher while on vacation in Paris, his sister exclaimed, "Fancy that!" The coincidence seemed so improbable that it left her both delighted and astonished.

Full Bottle

Definition: Being a "full bottle" of something means being knowledgeable or well-informed about that topic.

Example: On renewable energy, she was a whole bottle, able to discuss the latest technologies and policies confidently and sincerely.

Flash as a Rat with a Gold Tooth

Definition: Describing someone as "flash as a rat with a gold tooth" means they are showing off or looking flashy, often tacky or ostentatious.

Example: Dressed in his new, overly bright outfit, he was as flamboyant as a rat with a gold tooth, attracting attention and comments for his bold style.

Fair Go

Definition: "Fair go" is a plea for fairness or justice, asking for reasonable treatment or an opportunity to be heard or participate.

Example: When the minor team felt overshadowed in the competition, they asked for a fair go, wanting an equal chance to showcase their skills and compete on level terms.

G

Galah

Definition: "Galah" means a foolish or silly person. It's named after a noisy, colorful Australian bird that loves to show off and make a lot of noise, just like someone acting silly.

Example: "Don't be such a galah," he chuckled, teasing his friend for making a harmless but silly mistake during the game. His friend had tripped over his own feet while trying to make a dramatic play, drawing laughter from everyone around.

Grog

Definition: "Grog" is a colloquial term for alcohol, particularly beer or spirits, in Australian slang. Historically, the term originated from the watered-down rum given to sailors in the British Navy. Today, it broadly refers to any alcoholic beverage, highlighting the integral role of casual drinking in Australian social culture.

Example: "We need to stock up on some grog for the party," the host mentioned, preparing for the upcoming celebration. They made a list of different beers and spirits to cater to all their guests' preferences, ensuring a well-stocked bar for the evening.

Gumtree

Definition: A "gumtree" is a tree native to Australia, typically a eucalyptus, and is an iconic part of the Australian natural landscape. Known for their towering height and distinctive peeling bark, gumtrees are a common sight in both urban and rural areas. They play a crucial role in the ecosystem, providing habitat for various wildlife, including koalas and birds.

Example: The backyard was shaded by a tall gumtree, its leaves rustling in the breeze and providing a perfect spot for relaxation. Under its expansive branches, the family set up a picnic, enjoying the cool shade and the gentle sounds of nature.

Goon

Definition: "Goon" is a slang term for cheap boxed wine, often associated with budget-friendly drinking options. It's a popular choice among students and those looking for an economical way to enjoy alcohol. The term reflects the casual and often humorous approach Australians have towards drinking culture.

Example: They bought a goon bag for the camping trip, opting for an affordable and easy-to-transport alcohol option. Around the campfire, they shared stories and laughter, the goon flowing freely as they enjoyed the simple pleasures of their outdoor adventure.

Gobsmacked

Definition: "Gobsmacked" means being amazed, astounded, or speechless, often due to surprise or shock. The term vividly captures the feeling of being completely taken aback by unexpected news or events.

Example: He was gobsmacked when he won the lottery, unable to believe his sudden change in fortune. As he stared at the winning ticket, he struggled to find the words to express his shock and joy.

Going Off

Definition: "Going off" can describe something very exciting or active and can also refer to food spoiling or going bad. When used to describe an event, it conveys a sense of high energy and enthusiasm. Conversely, when used in the context of food, it indicates that the item has deteriorated in quality and is no longer safe to consume.

Example: "The party was really going off," she recounted, describing the lively and energetic atmosphere where everyone was dancing and having a great time. Meanwhile, she also noticed some leftovers in the fridge that had started going off, emitting a sour smell.

Gnarly

Definition: "Gnarly" originally described something extreme or challenging, especially in surfing, but has come to mean something very difficult, intense, or bad. The term can be used positively to describe impressive feats, particularly in sports, or negatively to refer to unpleasant or tough situations.

Example: The waves were gnarly, presenting a challenging condition for even the most experienced surfers. As they paddled out, they knew they were in for a tough session, but the thrill of conquering such formidable waves was worth the effort.

Give it a Whirl

Definition: "Give it a whirl" means to try something or give it a go, showing a willingness to attempt something new. It reflects an open-minded and adventurous attitude, encouraging people to step out of their comfort zones and experience new activities.

Example: "I've never been on a horse before, but I'll give it a whirl," she said, eager to experience horseback riding. With a bit of instruction and a lot of excitement, she mounted the horse and set off on the trail, thrilled by the new experience.

Grab a Coldie

Definition: "Grab a coldie" means to get a cold beer, often used in social settings. It reflects the casual, relaxed approach Australians have toward sharing a drink.

Example: "After mowing the lawn, I'm going to grab a coldie," he said, looking forward to relaxing with a beer. He enjoyed it while chatting with his neighbor.

Gun

Definition: "Gun" is a slang term for someone very skilled or excellent in a particular area, often used in sports or other competitive fields. It signifies a high level of talent and proficiency, earning respect and admiration from others.

Example: "She's a real gun on the basketball court," commented the coach, impressed by her talent and skill. Her quick reflexes and sharp shooting made her a standout player, and she consistently led her team to victory.

G'day

Definition: "G'day" is a common Australian greeting, short for "Good Day," used informally to say hello. It embodies the friendly and relaxed demeanor typical of Australian interactions, making it a staple of everyday conversation.

Example: "G'day, mate, how's it going?" is a typical way to greet a friend in Australia, embodying the friendly and relaxed demeanor. The phrase instantly sets a welcoming tone, whether meeting someone for the first time or catching up with an old acquaintance.

<u>H</u>

Hit the Nail on the Head

Definition: This describes an action or explanation that is precisely accurate or correct. It acknowledges a person's pinpoint accuracy in addressing an issue.

Example: During the meeting, when Sarah suggested a solution to the budget discrepancy, her boss nodded approvingly, saying, "You've hit the nail on the head with that one, Sarah." Her insight had precisely targeted the core of the problem, earning her accolades from her peers.

Hoon

Definition: A hoon is a reckless driver who drives aggressively and dangerously.

Example: "That guy is such a hoon, always speeding and doing burnouts," the neighbor complained, shaking his head at the noisy car tearing down the street.

Hit the Hay

Definition: "Hit the hay" is a common expression to indicate going to bed or sleep. Though widely used beyond Australia, it colloquially marks the conclusion of the day's activities and the time to rest.

Example: Mark announced, "I'm ready to hit the hay after a long day of hiking and sightseeing," his exhaustion evident. He was asleep as soon as his head touched the pillow, fully embracing the restorative power of a good night's sleep.

Hump Day

Definition: "Hump day" refers to Wednesday, traditionally seen as the midpoint of the workweek. The term is used to signify getting over the "hump" of the week and the downhill progression towards the weekend.

Example: As they gathered around the water cooler, Jenny cheerfully reminded her colleagues, "Cheer up, everyone! It's hump day—we're halfway to the weekend!" Her words lifted the team's spirits, making the remainder of the week seem more bearable.

How Ya Going?

Definition: "How ya going?" is a standard Australian greeting, similar to "How are you?" or "How's it going?"

Example: "G'day mate, how ya going?" he greeted his friend, embodying the typical laid-back Aussie manner.

Hard Case

Definition: A hard case is someone funny or amusing, often known for their ability to entertain or make others laugh.

Example: "He's a real hard case, always making us laugh with his stories and jokes," she said, appreciating her witty friend.

Heaps

Definition: Heaps means a lot or a large quantity, used to emphasize abundance or excess.

Example: "I've got heaps of work to do before the weekend," she lamented, staring at her never-ending to-do list.

Heart of Gold

Definition: "Heart of gold" is an idiom that describes someone exceptionally kind and caring. It highlights an individual's deep-seated goodness or generosity, suggesting a noble and benevolent nature.

Example: Mr. Thompson, the elderly neighbor, always had time to listen and a smile to share. He genuinely had a heart of gold. His willingness to help and care for others made him a beloved figure in the community, and his kindness echoed through every interaction.

I

In the Same Boat

Definition: "In the same boat" describes being in a similar situation or facing the same problems. This idiom conveys a sense of shared experience or common plight, often used to highlight empathy or mutual understanding.

Example: During the team meeting, when frustrations about the new policy were voiced, the manager reassured everyone, saying, "We're all in the same boat here, and we'll work through these challenges together."

Icy Pole

Definition: An "icy polc" is a frozen treat on a stick, similar to a popsicle. It is widely enjoyed as a refreshing snack, especially in hot Australian weather.

Example: On a scorching summer day, the kids clamored for icy poles, the frosty treats providing a delightful escape from the relentless heat.

In the Nick

Definition: "In the nick" means arriving or accomplishing something just in time, often highlighting scenarios where timing is crucial.

Example: He arrived just in time for the meeting, sliding into his seat just as the presentation's first slide was displayed.

I'll Be Buggered

Definition: "I'll be buggered" is an Australian expression of surprise or disbelief, similar to saying "I can't believe it!"

Example: "Well, I'll be buggered; they won the game!" he exclaimed, his voice filled with astonishment over the team's unexpected victory.

In the Red

Definition: "In the red" denotes a financial status where expenses exceed income, used to describe accounts or businesses operating at a loss.

Example: The report showed that, despite increased sales, the company was still in the red, prompting discussions on cost-cutting measures to improve financial health.

In the Doghouse

Definition: The phrase "In the doghouse" is used to describe a situation where someone is in trouble or has upset another person, leading to them being in a difficult position.

Example: Since forgetting her birthday, he's been in the doghouse. His efforts to make amends have yet to restore their usual cheerful rapport.

I Reckon

Definition: "I reckon" is a phrase equivalent to "I think" or "I believe," commonly used in casual conversation in Australia.

Example: "I reckon we should go to the movies tonight," she suggested, offering a relaxing plan for the evening.

I'm Knackered

Definition: "I'm knackered" means feeling exhausted or tired, indicating a strong need for rest.

Example: After the lengthy bike ride, he collapsed onto the couch, declaring, "I'm knackered," his energy was completely spent.

In the Dunny

Definition: "In the dunny" means being in the toilet or bathroom, with "dunny" being a colloquial Australian term for a lavatory.

Example: "Where's Dave?" "He's in the dunny," his friend replied, indicating he was momentarily occupied in the restroom.

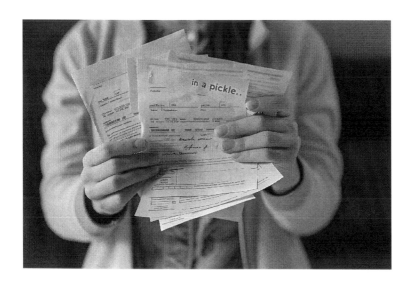

In a Pickle

Definition: "In a pickle" means being in a difficult situation or dilemma, often involving a tough decision or complex problem.

Example: "I'm in a pickle; I don't know which job offer to accept," she confided, torn between two promising opportunities.

In Your Element

Definition: Being "in your element" means feeling exceptionally comfortable and confident in a particular situation or activity where one is likely to perform at their best.

Example: On stage, with the spotlight shining down, she was clearly in her element, her voice soaring as she sang with evident passion and skill.

J

Jaffle

Definition: A jaffle is a toasted sandwich made in a special jaffle iron. The iron seals the edges and creates a pocket of deliciousness, often with savory fillings.

Example: On a cold winter's night, they made cheese and tomato jaffles, and the hot, melted sandwiches provided comfort and warmth.

Jumbuck

Definition: Jumbuck is an Australian term for a sheep, often used in traditional songs and folklore.

Example: The iconic song "Waltzing Matilda" mentions a jumbuck, embedding the word into Australian cultural heritage as a symbol of rural life.

Joey

Definition: A joey is a baby kangaroo or wallaby, often seen peeking out from its mother's pouch.

Example: At the wildlife park, visitors were delighted to see a joey, its curious eyes observing the world from the safety of its mother's pouch.

Just Down the Road

Definition: "Just down the road" means nearby or a short distance away, used to indicate that a location is not far.

Example: "The new café? It's just down the road, about five minutes' walk from here," explained the locals, highlighting the convenience of the place.

Jiffy

Definition: A jiffy is an informal term that is used for a concise amount of time, suggesting something will happen almost immediately.

Example: "I'll be ready in a jiffy," she called out as she finished getting dressed for the outing, indicating she would be done very soon.

Jug

Definition: A jug is a pitcher or large container for holding and pouring liquids, such as water or juice.

Example: They kept a jug of iced lemonade on the table during the barbecue, offering a refreshing drink to beat the heat.

Journo

Definition: Journo is a colloquial term for a journalist, often used informally in conversation or writing.

Example: The local journo covered the story of the community festival, capturing the vibrant events and people's stories.

Jack of All Trades

Definition: A "jack of all trades" is someone skilled in many different areas and capable of performing various types of work or tasks.

Example: With his wide range of skills, from carpentry to electronics, he was considered a jack of all trades, always ready to tackle any job.

Jelly

Definition: Jelly in Australian English can refer to a gelatin dessert, similar to what is known as 'Jell-O' in North America, or colloquially, it can refer to jellyfish in beach-related contexts.

Example: At the picnic, the kids were excited about the dessert, a fruity jelly set into fun shapes. Meanwhile, at the beach, swimmers were cautious of jelly sightings, not wanting a sting to ruin their day.

Jam-Packed

Definition: "Jam-packed" refers to a situation where a place or event is highly crowded or complete, often to the point where there is hardly any room to move. This term is commonly used in Australia to describe venues or situations overflowing with people or items.

Example: The concert was jam-packed, with fans filling every space to glimpse their favorite band. The energy was electric; the crowd squeezed together, each person reveling in the shared excitement of the live music experience.

Jack Up

Definition: "Jack up" means to raise or increase something, like prices or expectations, and can also refer to organizing or arranging an event or agreement.

Example: Consumers were frustrated when the supermarket jacked up the prices of essential goods without warning.

K

Kelpie

Definition: A Kelpie is a breed of Australian sheepdog, renowned for it's herding abilities and intelligence. You'll find them across Australian farms, managing livestock and their performing complex tasks.

Example: As the sun dipped below the horizon, the kelpie sprang into action, skillfully herding the scattered sheep into the pen. Its focused gaze and precise movements showcased not only its rigorous training but also its natural instincts, honed through generations of selective breeding.

Kindie

Definition: "Kindie" is a colloquial Australian term for kindergarten, referring to the early childhood educational setting for young children. It marks the start of a child's formal education and is a place where foundational skills are developed through play and structured activities.

Example: "My daughter starts kindie next week," shared a parent with a mix of excitement and nervousness, reflecting on the significant milestone of her child stepping into a new world of learning and social interaction.

Knocker

Definition: A "knocker" is someone known for their tendency to criticize or complain about almost everything, without constructive intent. It describes a person who is quick to find faults and slow to acknowledge positives.

Example: Known throughout the town as the perennial knocker, he never missed an opportunity to voice his dissatisfaction about the local events and initiatives, especially to the community who worked hard to organize them.

Kick the Bucket

Definition: "Kick the bucket" is an informal and somewhat humorous idiom used to refer to dying. The phrase is often used light-heartedly to discuss death in a way that reduces its gravitas.

Example: He often joked that he wouldn't kick the bucket until he had witnessed his beloved team clinch the championship, a testament to his unwavering support and lifelong dedication as a fan.

Kick into Gear

Definition: "Kick into gear" refers to starting to operate effectively or becoming more active and energetic. This phrase is often used in Australia to suggest initiating action or significantly improving performance in a work, sporting, or personal context.

Example: With the project deadline fast approaching, the team really kicked into gear, their productivity and energy levels soaring. Meetings became more focused, ideas flowed freely, and everyone contributed vigorously, determined to deliver outstanding results on time.

Keep the Bastards Honest

Definition: "Keep the bastards honest" is a phrase commonly used in Australian political and business contexts, advocating for vigilance and accountability among those in positions of power. It emphasizes the need for transparency and integrity among leaders.

Example: The investigative journalist viewed her role as crucial to keeping the bastards honest, tirelessly working to expose corruption and ensure politicians lived up to their promises and duties.

Knee-High to a Grasshopper

Definition: The idiom "knee-high to a grasshopper" is used to describe being very young or notably small, often in a nostalgic recount of childhood. It paints a picture of a time when one was as tiny as being only as tall as a grasshopper's knee.

Example: "I've known you since you were knee-high to a grasshopper," remarked the elderly man to the young adult, his voice tinged with affection as he recalled the many years they had known each other, from the young man's early childhood to his current successes.

Kettle

Definition: In figurative usage, a "kettle" refers to a group of people engaged in noisy, often trivial or gossip-filled discussions, similar to the bubbling and simmering of water in a kettle.

Example: "Don't mind him; he's just stirring the kettle," remarked someone as they observed their colleague mingling, spreading rumors and stirring up drama much like the steam rising from a kettle.

Kookaburra

Definition: The kookaburra is a native Australian bird, famous for its distinctive, laughter-like call that echoes through the forests at dawn and dusk. This bird is a beloved symbol of the Australian bush.

Example: As dawn broke, the laughter of kookaburras filled the air, a familiar and comforting sound that heralded the start of another day in the lush Australian landscape.

Knock Off

Definition: "Knock off" is an informal Australian expression meaning to finish work or cease working, particularly at the end of a workday.

Example: "Let's knock off early today and go for a drink," the boss suggested, recognizing the team's hard work throughout the week and proposing a well-deserved early start to their weekend relaxation.

Keen as a Bean

Definition: "Keen as a bean" is a lively and informal Australian expression used to describe someone who is extremely enthusiastic or eager about doing something. The idiom draws a playful comparison to a bean, suggesting a bouncy and vibrant energy.

Example: When the opportunity to volunteer at the international film festival was announced, Mia was keen as a bean, immediately signing up for multiple shifts. Her excitement was palpable, and her readiness to dive into the experience epitomized her boundless zest for exploring new cultural events.

Keep at Bay

Definition: "Keep at bay" is an expression used to describe the act of preventing something or someone from approaching or exerting influence. In Australian parlance, it particularly means maintaining a safe distance from potential trouble or danger, whether literal or figurative.

Example: As the clouds gathered and the sky darkened, the campers took all necessary precautions to keep the impending storm at bay. By securing their tents and safeguarding their supplies, they managed to avoid the worst of the weather, ensuring their safety and comfort through proactive measures.

L

Like a Rat up a Drainpipe

Definition: This idiom describes someone doing something very quickly or eagerly, akin to the swift movement of a rat.

Example: When the doors opened for the sale, shoppers went in like rats up a drainpipe, eager to grab the best deals.

Like Water off a Duck's Back

Definition: This phrase means being unaffected by criticism or negative comments, similar to water easily rolling off a duck's back.

Example: Despite the harsh feedback, the criticisms were like water off a duck's back to her, never dampening her spirit or confidence.

Lay-by

Definition: Lay-by is a payment plan where customers can reserve goods and pay for them over time, receiving the item once fully paid.

Example: She put the expensive coat on lay-by, paying it off in installments until she could proudly take it home.

Laid-Back

Definition: Laid-back describes a person or environment that is relaxed, easygoing, and free from stress or hurry.

Example: The beach town had a laid-back vibe, its residents living life at a leisurely pace, enjoying the sun and surf without the rush of city life.

Loo

Definition: Loo is an informal term for the toilet or bathroom, commonly used in Australia.

Example: "Where's the loo?" the tourist asked, in need of directions to the nearest restroom.

Lollies

Definition: "Lollies" is a term used in Australian English to refer to sweets or candy. This encompasses a wide variety of sugary treats, from hard candies to gummies and chocolates. The term is particularly beloved by children and often used in discussions about treats, snacks, or desserts.

Example: At the party, the kids were most excited about the large bowl of lollies set out on the dessert table. Their eyes lit up as they picked their favorite types, filling small bags with a colorful assortment of sugary delights to enjoy during the celebration.

Lippy

Definition: Lippy is an informal term for lipstick or lip balm, commonly used in casual conversation.

Example: "Can you lend me your lippy?" she asked her friend, wanting to touch up her makeup.

Lend Me Your Ear

Definition: "Lend me your ear" is a polite request in Australian communication asking someone to give their attention and listen carefully. It's derived from classical rhetoric but remains widely used to signify the importance of the forthcoming message.

Example: "Lend me your ear for a moment," the manager began, gathering the team to share some critical updates. Her tone suggested the importance of her words, encouraging everyone to focus intently on her message.

M

Maccas

Definition: Maccas is the Australian slang term for McDonald's, the popular fast-food chain.

Example: "Let's grab some brekkie at Maccas," suggested Liam, craving their famous McMuffins to start the day.

Mozzie

Definition: Mozzie is the Australian term for mosquito, often used in discussions about the pesky insects, especially during summer.

Example: Camping by the river was lovely, except for the swarms of mozzies that emerged at dusk.

Mum's the Word

Definition: "Mum's the word" means to keep something secret or confidential, emphasizing the importance of silence or discretion.

Example: After planning the surprise party, they all agreed, "Mum's the word," to ensure the guest of honor remained unaware.

Moolah

Definition: Moolah is a slang term for money or cash, used in casual conversation to discuss finances or costs.

Example: We need to earn and save some more moolah if we want to go on that trip!

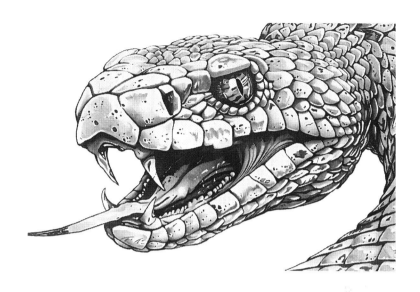

Mad as a Cut Snake

Definition: Being "mad as a cut snake" means extremely angry or upset, using vivid imagery to convey intense emotions.

Example: When he saw the damage to his car, he was as mad as a cut snake, furious about the carelessness of the other driver.

Middy

Definition: A middy is a medium-sized glass of beer in Australia, usually holding about half a pint.

Example: At the pub, he ordered a middy, preferring a smaller drink so he could enjoy different varieties of beer.

Mint

Definition: Mint is a slang term meaning excellent or in perfect condition, often used to describe something that is top-notch or as good as new.

Example: "This vintage guitar is absolutely mint," admired the collector, appreciating its pristine state and quality.

Mong

Definition: Mong is a derogatory term used to describe someone acting foolish or unpleasant, and it should be used with caution due to its offensive nature.

Example: "Don't be a mong," someone might say, criticizing another's behavior, though it's important to be mindful of the term's potentially hurtful connotation.

Make a Pig's Ear of Something

Definition: "Make a pig's ear of something" means to do something badly or make a mess of a task. In Australian usage, it implies handling something poorly, often leading to mistakes or failure.

Example: He really made a pig's ear of the kitchen renovation; nothing was installed correctly, and it all had to be redone by a professional.

Muck Up

Definition: To muck up means to make a mistake or mess up something, often leading to a problematic or undesirable outcome.

Example: I really mucked up that recipe. My cake ended up more like a pancake in thickness.

Muck Around

Definition: To muck around means to waste time or goof off, often in a playful or unproductive manner.

Example: "Stop mucking around and focus on your homework," the mother chided her children, urging them to take their studies seriously.

My Shout

Definition: "My shout" indicates that it's one's turn to pay, usually for a round of drinks at a bar. In Australia, this phrase is a common way to offer to cover the cost in a social setting, showing generosity and camaraderie.

Example: "Don't worry about this round; it's my shout," he declared at the pub, reaching for his wallet as his mates thanked him for the beers.

Mickey Mouse

Definition: Describing something as "Mickey Mouse" means it is small-scale, unimportant, or not very serious. Australians might use this term to criticize an operation or activity that lacks professionalism or significance.

Example: The project felt a bit Mickey Mouse, lacking the rigorous planning and serious investment it needed to truly succeed. They all agreed that a more professional approach was necessary.

Make Ends Meet

Definition: "Make ends meet" means managing one's financial resources carefully to just cover essential expenses. In the Australian context, it often refers to maintaining financial stability through careful budgeting, especially in times of limited means.

Example: After the recent cut in hours at work, she had to tighten her budget considerably to make ends meet, and prioritize rent and groceries compared to her wants.

Mouth Off

Definition: To "mouth off" means to speak loudly and boastfully or to complain without restraint. In Australian slang, it describes talking arrogantly, rudely, or making loud, often unwelcome comments.

Example: He started to mouth off about the new policies in the office, airing his grievances loudly in the break room without considering how it might affect his coworkers.

<u>N</u>

No Worries/No Wakkas

Definition: "No worries" is an expression meaning "it's okay" or "no problem," commonly used in Australia to reassure someone or dismiss concerns.
Example: When she apologized for being late, he replied, "No worries," indicating that it wasn't an issue and all was forgiven.

Nappy

Definition: Nappy is the Australian term for a diaper, used for infants and young children.

Example: Packing for the day out, she made sure to include plenty of nappies in the baby bag, prepared for any situation.

Nick Off

Definition: "Nick off" is an informal command telling someone to go away or leave, similar to "get lost" or "buzz off."

Example: Frustrated with the interruption, she told the onlooker to nick off, wanting some privacy to handle the situation.

Nippy

Definition: "Nippy" refers to weather or air that is sharply cold or chilly, often implying a biting quality to the coldness.

Example: "Make sure to wear a coat; it's quite nippy outside," the mother advised her children as they prepared to leave for school.

Nugget

Definition: A nugget is a small piece or chunk of something, often used to describe a valuable find, like gold, or a solid piece of advice.

Example: Panning in the stream, he was thrilled to find a small gold nugget, a shiny reward for his efforts.

No-Brainer

Definition: A "no-brainer" is a decision or choice that is extremely easy to make, as the best course of action is obvious and requires little to no deliberation.

Example: For Jack, deciding to buy tickets to the football final was a no-brainer, given his lifelong support for the team and their rare appearance in the championship game.

Noggin

Definition: "Noggin" is a playful and informal term for the head or skull. It's often used in a light-hearted context, especially when cautioning someone about potential bumps or accidents.

Example: "Watch your noggin as you duck under that branch," he called out to his hiking companion, concerned about the low-hanging obstacle on the forest trail.

Nan and Pop

Definition: "Nan and Pop" are endearing terms used in Australia to refer to grandparents. These terms convey warmth and familial affection, often associated with fond childhood memories.

Example: The children's faces lit up with joy as they arrived at Nan and Pop's house, eagerly anticipating a weekend filled with storytelling, baking, and games.

Nab

Definition: To "nab" means to grab, capture, or steal something, typically in a swift or secretive manner.

Example: The police officer managed to nab the suspect just as he was trying to flee the scene, ensuring that he was held accountable for his actions.

Not My Cup of Tea

Definition: "Not my cup of tea" is a phrase used to express disinterest or dislike towards something. It indicates that the subject is not to one's taste or preference.

Example: While everyone else was excited about the horror movie marathon, he admitted that scary films were not his cup of tea and opted for a quieter evening at home.

Night Owl

Definition: A "night owl" is someone who prefers staying up late or is most active and alert during the night-time.

Example: Being a night owl, she enjoyed the calm and solitude of working late into the night, finding her creativity peaked when the world around her was quiet.

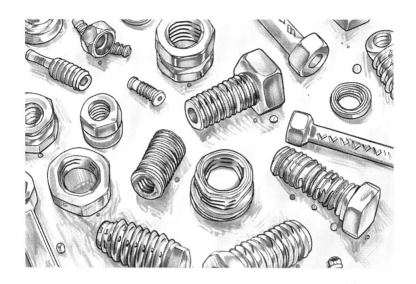

Nuts and Bolts

Definition: The "nuts and bolts" of something refer to its basic, essential components. This phrase is often used to discuss the fundamental, practical details of a project or situation.

Example: In the meeting, they decided to skip the theoretical discussions and focus on the nuts and bolts of the event planning, ensuring every critical task was assigned and timelines were clear.

Not Batting an Eyelid

Definition: "Not batting an eyelid" means showing no emotional reaction, surprise, or concern in situations where such responses might be expected.

Example: Despite the chaos unfolding at the airport with flight delays and cancellations, she did not bat an eyelid, calmly reading her book and waiting for her eventual boarding call.

O

Outback

Definition: The Outback refers to the remote and rural areas of Australia, especially the arid desert regions known for their rugged terrain and sparse population.

Example: They embarked on a journey through the Outback, experiencing the vast, unspoiled landscapes and the tough but rewarding lifestyle of its inhabitants.

Oz

Definition: Oz is a shortened, informal term for Australia, often used affectionately by Australians and others.
Example: "Can't wait to return to Oz and hit the beach," remarked the traveler, eagerly anticipating their return to Australia's sunny shores.

Ozzie

Definition: Ozzie is an informal term for an Australian person, embodying the friendly and informal nature of Australian culture.
Example: She's an Ozzie through and through (entirely), known for her laid-back attitude, love of barbies, and passion for cricket.

Old Mate

Definition: Old mate is a term used to refer to someone whose name you don't remember or know, often used in storytelling or conversation.
Example: "I ran into old mate from school yesterday; haven't seen him in years!" said Jack, referring to a former classmate whose name he couldn't recall.

On the Nose

Definition: "On the nose" describes something that is unpopular or disliked, often because it is considered in poor taste or offensive.
Example: The politician's comments were really on the nose, causing a public backlash and demands for an apology.

Off Your Chops

Definition: "Off your chops" means intoxicated or under the influence of drugs, used to describe someone who is visibly affected by substances.

Example: After the party, it was clear he was off his chops, barely able to stand or speak coherently.

Out of Whack

Definition: "Out of whack" means not functioning correctly or being out of order, often used to describe something that is disorganized or malfunctioning.

Example: "My computer's completely out of whack; I might need to call IT support," complained the employee, struggling with the malfunctioning device.

Out on the Piss / On the Piss

Definition: "Out on the piss" is a colloquial way of saying out drinking alcohol, often with the intention of a heavy drinking session.

Example: They were planning to go out on the piss this weekend, looking forward to unwinding with friends at the local pubs and bars.

On the Blower

Definition: "On the blower" is slang term for talking on the telephone, originating from the early days of old telephone designs."

Example: "Can't talk now; I'm on the blower with the boss," he said, indicating he was in the middle of an important phone call.

Out of Pocket

Definition: The term "out of pocket" typically refers to spending money or incurring expenses, often resulting in a temporary financial loss. It can also indicate a person being unreachable or acting unnaturally. When used in the context of spending money, it means that the individual is making a payment using their own funds.

Example: After the holiday shopping spree, she was significantly out of pocket, having spent much more than intended. "Dad said something totally out of pocket the other day."

Over the Moon

Definition: "Over the moon" describes feeling extremely happy or delighted, often in response to a positive event or outcome.
Example: She was over the moon about her promotion, her joy and excitement palpable as she shared the news with her family.

On the Job

Definition: "On the job" means working or engaged in one's duties, often used to signify that someone is currently busy with work-related tasks.
Example: He's currently on the job and unavailable to take the call, as he is fully focused on finishing the project before the deadline.

On the Wallaby Track

Definition: "On the wallaby track" refers to wandering or traveling without a fixed route or job, often in search of work. This phrase has historical roots in Australia, traditionally associated with itinerant workers moving from place to place in search of employment or better opportunities.

Example: After losing his job in the city, he decided to go on the wallaby track, taking up temporary jobs as he traveled through the countryside.

Over the Top

Definition: "Over the top" describes something that is excessive, exaggerated, or beyond what is considered normal or appropriate.

Example: Her birthday party was over the top, complete with fireworks, a live band, and a gourmet buffet, far surpassing the usual celebration.

On the Ball

Definition: "On the ball" means being alert, attentive, and quick to understand or react, indicating competence and the ability to stay focused.
Example: You need to be on the ball in this fast-paced industry, always ready to respond to changes and challenges.

Out on a Limb

Definition: "Out on a limb" describes being in a risky or isolated position. This idiom is commonly used in Australia to convey a situation where someone is left vulnerable or in a precarious position, both literally and metaphorically.
Example: By advocating for a controversial policy change, the politician found himself out on a limb, with colleagues willing to publicly support his stance.

On the Dole

Definition: "On the dole" refers to receiving unemployment benefits from the government. In Australia, this term is used to describe individuals who are collecting financial assistance because they are currently out of work.
Example: Since being made redundant, he has been on the dole, relying on the weekly payments to cover his basic expenses while he searches for new employment opportunities.

Out of the Woods

Definition: "Out of the woods" means no longer being in danger or difficulty. In Australian usage, this idiom indicates that someone has successfully navigated through a challenging situation or problem and is now in a safer or more stable position.

Example: After months of treatment, the doctor finally gave her the good news that she was out of the woods, her health much improved and the risk significantly reduced.

On the Money

Definition: "On the money" means accurate or correct, often used to describe a statement, prediction, or assessment that is exactly right.

Example: His prediction about the election results was on the money, proving his expertise and insight into the political landscape.

P

Prawns

Definition: Prawns in Australian English refer to what is commonly known as shrimp in other countries, a staple in Australian seafood cuisine.

Example: "Throw another prawn on the barbie" is a famous phrase, epitomizing the Australian love for grilling seafood outdoors.

Prezzie

Definition: Prezzie is an informal term for a present or gift, often used in casual conversation.

Example: For her birthday, she received lots of prezzies from friends and family, each one wrapped in bright, cheerful paper.

Pig's Arse

Definition: "Pig's arse" is an expression of disbelief or disagreement, similar to saying "I don't believe it" or "That's not true."

Example: When he claimed he could run a marathon without any training, his mate retorted, "Pig's arse! You'd be lucky to run five kilometers."

Pash

Definition: Pash is slang for a passionate kiss, often used among younger people to describe making out.

Example: The couple shared a quick pash in the alley, their goodbye filled with longing and affection.

Pissing Down

Definition: "Pissing down" is a crude but vivid colloquial term in Australian English for raining very heavily. The expression conveys the intensity and relentlessness of the rainfall.

Example: As they looked out the window, the rain was pissing down, sheets of water blurring the scenery and dashing any hopes of an outdoor barbecue.

Piss Off

Definition: "Piss off" is a blunt command telling someone to go away or leave, often used in anger or irritation.

Example: Frustrated with the constant teasing, she told her brother to piss off, wanting some peace and quiet.

Piss Poor

Definition: "Piss poor" is an Australian slang term used to describe something that is of very low quality or extremely unsatisfactory. The term is derogatory and conveys a strong disapproval of the standard or performance of something.

Example: The performance of the team this season has been piss poor, with fans and critics alike expressing their disappointment at the lack of effort and skill displayed in the games.

Pint

Definition: A pint is a large glass or serving of beer, typically 0.15005 Gallons (568 mL) a standard size in Australian bars.

Example: After a long day, a cold pint at the local pub was exactly what he needed to unwind and relax.

Punter

Definition: A punter in Australia refers to a person who gambles, especially one who bets on races or sporting events.

Example: The racecourse was filled with punters, each studying the form guide and placing bets on their chosen horses.

Packed to the Rafters

Definition: "Packed to the rafters" is an idiom used in Australia to describe a place so extremely crowded or full that it seems like it's going to burst. This phrase is often used to depict venues or homes overflowing with people or items.

Example: The concert hall was packed to the rafters, fans squeezing in to catch a glimpse of their favorite band. The energy was palpable, with every available space filled with eager concert-goers.

Piss-Up

Definition: A piss-up is a colloquial term for a party or gathering where a significant amount of alcohol is consumed.

Example: The office Christmas party turned into a real piss-up, with everyone letting loose and enjoying the festive spirit.

Pissed

Definition: Pissed is a slang term for being drunk or intoxicated, commonly used in Australian English.

Example: By the end of the night, he was so pissed that he could barely stand, needing help from his friends to get home.

Piss Around

Definition: To piss around means to waste time or fool around, not taking things seriously or procrastinating.

Example: "We can't afford to piss around with this deadline approaching," the project leader stated, urging the team to focus and work efficiently.

Pokies

Definition: Pokies are poker machines or slot machines, commonly found in casinos and pubs across Australia.

Example: He spent the evening playing the pokies, hoping for a big win but mostly just enjoying the thrill of the game.

Pass the Buck

Definition: "Pass the buck" means to shift responsibility or blame to someone else. In Australian usage, this phrase signifies the act of avoiding taking responsibility by making someone else handle the problem.

Example: When the project failed, the team leader tried to pass the buck to his subordinates, but it was clear that the oversight had been at all levels.

Pluggers

Definition: "Pluggers are another name for Flip-flops or thongs in Australia." Made typically from rubber, these inexpensive sandals are favored for their comfort and simplicity, ideal for beach wear or informal settings.

Example: Wearing his pluggers, he strolled along the beach, feeling the soft rubber providing comfort as the sand sifted between his toes.

Piss in One's Pocket

Definition: "Piss in one's pocket" is an Australian expression used to describe the act of giving excessive flattery, often for personal gain. The phrase suggests insincerity and the intention of ingratiating oneself with someone else.

Example: He could tell his colleague was just trying to piss in his pocket with all the compliments during the meeting, likely aiming to get his support for the upcoming project proposal.

Pull Your Finger Out

Definition: "Pull your finger out" is a direct Australian expression urging someone to stop wasting time and start being productive. It's a call to action, often used when someone is perceived as being lazy or procrastinating.

Example: The manager told the team to pull their fingers out and finish the project by the deadline, emphasizing that time was running out and there was no room for delay.

Q

Quokka

Definition: The quokka is a small, friendly-looking marsupial native to Western Australia, known for its photogenic smile and lack of fear of humans. **Example:** Tourists flock to Rottnest Island to see the quokkas, snapping selfies with the adorable creatures that seem always to be smiling.

Quote

Definition: To quote means to provide a price estimate or offer for a service or product, detailing the cost involved.

Example: The contractor came to quote for the kitchen renovation, laying out the expenses for materials and labor.

Quiet as a Mouse

Definition: "Quiet as a mouse" is an expression used to describe someone or something making very little noise, being extremely quiet or silent.

Example: During the library study session, everyone was quiet as a mouse, focused on their books and notes without a sound.

R

Right Off the Bat

Definition: "Right off the bat" means immediately or from the very beginning. This phrase, used in Australia and other English-speaking countries, indicates taking prompt action or addressing something directly and without delay.

Example: Right off the bat, she impressed the interview panel with her clear vision and detailed plan for the department.

Ripper

Definition: Ripper is an Australian slang term meaning excellent, fantastic, or awesome, often used to express approval or enthusiasm.

Example: "That was a ripper of a match!" exclaimed the fan, thrilled by the exciting game they had just witnessed.

Roo

Definition: Roo is a common abbreviation for kangaroo, an iconic Australian animal, often used in everyday speech.

Example: While driving through the countryside, they spotted a roo hopping across the fields, an everyday Australian sight.

Reckon

Definition: Reckon is a verb meaning to think or believe, commonly used in Australian English in place of "think" or "believe."

Example: "I reckon it's going to rain later," he predicted, observing the darkening clouds on the horizon.

Run of the Mill

Definition: "Run of the mill" describes something that is ordinary, typical, or unexceptional. This term in Australia is used to denote something that is average or standard, without any distinguishing features or qualities.

Example: The movie was pretty run of the mill-just your average romantic comedy with the usual plot twists and predictable ending.

Ratbag

Definition: Ratbag refers to a mischievous or troublesome person, often used humorously or affectionately to describe someone who behaves badly but endearingly.

Example: The youngest child was the family ratbag, always getting into scrapes but charming everyone with his cheeky grin.

Rough as Guts

Definition: "Rough as guts" describes something very rough, crude, or unrefined, often used to characterize a place, person, or situation lacking in sophistication or polish.

Example: The old tavern was as rough as guts, with its dilapidated decor and rowdy patrons, but it had a certain charm that appealed to the regulars.

Rip-Off

Definition: A rip-off is something that is overpriced or an unfair deal, where the cost greatly exceeds the value or quality of the item or service.

Example: "That restaurant is a total rip-off," complained the customer, feeling cheated by the high prices and mediocre food.

Righto

Definition: Righto is an informal way of saying "okay" or "alright," indicating agreement or acknowledgment.

Example: "Righto, I'll see you at six then," he agreed, confirming the meeting time with a friend.

Rock Up

Definition: To rock up means to arrive or appear at a location, often without a formal arrangement or specific time.

Example: "Just rock up when you feel like it; we'll be here all day," invited the host, offering a flexible and laid-back approach to the gathering.

Rego

Definition: Rego is a slang term for vehicle registration, referring to the official process of registering a car or other vehicle with the authorities.

Example: "I need to renew my rego before the end of the month," she remembered, noting the impending deadline for her car's registration.

Rubber

Definition: In Australian English, "rubber" commonly refers to an eraser used to remove pencil marks from paper. This term highlights the difference in terminology between Australian and American English, where the American equivalent is simply "eraser."

Example: During the exam, Sarah realized she had made a mistake in her calculations. She quickly reached for her rubber, rubbing away the lead.

Rough End of the Pineapple

Definition: "Rough end of the pineapple" is an Australian idiom used to describe getting a bad deal or experiencing the worst part of a situation. It suggests encountering the less favorable or more difficult aspects of a circumstance.

Example: When the company layoffs were announced, it was clear he got the rough end of the pineapple, losing his job despite years of dedicated service.

Rubbish Bin

Definition: A "rubbish bin" is the container in which trash is placed. In Australian households, workplaces, and public spaces, these bins are essential for waste management and are regularly collected by local waste services.

Example: After finishing their snacks at the park, the family made sure to throw all the wrappers and leftover food into the nearby rubbish bin.

Rack Off

Definition: "Rack off" is a directive telling someone to go away or leave, used in a dismissive or irritated manner.

Example: Frustrated with the uninvited guest, she told him to rack off, wanting to end the unwelcome intrusion.

S

Serviette

Definition: In Australia, a "serviette" refers to a paper napkin used at the dining table. In other countries people often refer to as a "napkin."

Example: At the outdoor picnic, the hostess made sure to place a stack of serviettes on each table, allowing guests to easily clean their hands and faces as they enjoyed the assortment of finger foods and barbecue treats. The serviettes were not only practical but also featured colorful designs, adding a festive touch to the setting.

Sunnies

Definition: "Sunnies" is a popular Australian slang term for sunglasses.

Example: Before hitting the beach, Jenna grabbed her towel, sunscreen, and her favorite pair of sunnies. Wearing them, she strolled along the sand, protected from the harsh sun while enjoying the vibrant seaside scenery.

Salvo

Definition: Salvo is an informal term for the Salvation Army, often used in the context of their charity shops and community services.

Example: "I picked up this jacket at the Salvo store," he mentioned, praising the quality and bargain he found at the charity shop.

Snag

Definition: Snag is another term for a sausage, especially when cooked on a barbecue, very common in Australian gatherings.

Example: "Let's throw a few snags on the barbie," suggested the host, preparing for the everyday Australian cookout.

Swag

Definition: Swag refers to a bundle of belongings or a bedroll used by campers, also known as a portable sleeping unit.

Example: He unrolled his swag under the stars, the simple bedding synonymous with the outdoor, nomadic lifestyle in Australia.

Sheila

Definition: Sheila is an informal term for a woman or girl, though it can be considered outdated or derogatory in modern contexts.

Example: "She's a great sheila," he said, using the old-fashioned term to compliment a woman he admired.

Sanga

Definition: Sanga is an informal term for a sandwich, a common item in Australian lunches.

Example: "I've packed a chicken sanga for lunch," said the worker, looking forward to his homemade sandwich at break time.

Servo

Definition: Servo is an informal term for a service station or gas station in Australia.

Example: "We'll stop at the next servo to fuel up and grab some snacks," planned the driver on their road trip.

Schooner

Definition: A schooner is a type of beer glass or serving of beer, typically around 9.6 oz (285mL) in some Australian states, smaller than a pint.

Example: In the pub, he ordered a schooner, the perfect size for trying different beers without getting too full.

Stubby

Definition: A stubby is a small bottle of beer, typically 12.6803 oz (375m, a popular size in Australia.

Example: On a hot day, there's nothing like cracking open a cold stubby to quench your thirst, the small bottle perfect for a quick drink.

Stubbie Holder

Definition: A stubbie holder is an insulated holder used to keep beer bottles cold, a common accessory at Australian picnics and barbecues.

Example: He pulled his beer from the stubbie holder, appreciating how it kept the drink chilled even on a hot day.

Soft Drink

Definition: In Australia, the term "soft drink" generally refers to carbonated beverages like cola, lemon-lime drinks, and other flavored fizzy drinks. This term is commonly used across the country, though regional variations such as "soda" or "fizzy drink" may also be heard.

Example: At the barbecue, the cooler was stocked with a variety of soft drinks, from classic cola to zesty ginger beer.

Sook

Definition: A sook is someone who is perceived as easily upset, sensitive, or overly emotional.

Example: "Don't be such a sook," teased his sister when he complained about the playful splash in the pool.

Shazza

Definition: Shazza is a common nickname for Sharon, often used affectionately or informally.

Example: "Shazza's throwing a party this weekend," her friends mentioned, using the familiar nickname to refer to her.

Spa

Definition: In Australian slang, "spa" refers to a hot tub or jacuzzi, emphasizing its use for relaxation and socializing. It is commonly mentioned in leisure activities or amenities at resorts and homes.

Example: "Let's jump in the spa and unwind," suggested Emma after a long day of hiking. The warm, bubbling water was perfect for relaxing and enjoying the cool evening under the stars.

Scratchie

Definition: A scratchie is a scratch card or instant lottery ticket, where you scratch off a thin film to reveal if you've won a prize.

Example: She bought a scratchie on a whim and couldn't believe her luck when she won a small prize.

Surfie

Definition: A surfie is someone who enjoys surfing, often spending a lot of time at the beach catching waves.

Example: The surfies were out every morning, chasing the best breaks and embodying the beach-centric lifestyle.

Smoko

Definition: Smoko is a break from work, traditionally for a smoke or snack, but now more broadly means any kind of break time.

Example: "Let's take a smoko," suggested the foreman, giving the workers time to rest and recharge during a busy day.

Slab

Definition: A slab is a case of beer, typically containing 24 cans or bottles, commonly purchased for parties or gatherings.
Example: "We'll need at least a slab for the barbecue on Saturday," he calculated, planning for the thirsty crowd expected at the event.

Staunch

Definition: "Staunch" is a term used to describe the act of stopping or confronting someone abruptly, typically in a forceful or assertive manner.
Example: The journalist staunched the politician outside the parliament, unleashing a barrage of challenging questions. Caught off guard, the politician scrambled to respond, the sudden confrontation exemplifying the high-stakes nature of political journalism.

Suss

Definition: To suss something out means to investigate or examine it, often to understand it better or figure out a solution.
Example: "I need to suss out why the computer keeps crashing," said the IT specialist, determined to solve the issue.

Spit the Dummy

Definition: "Spit the dummy" is an Australian phrase used to describe someone throwing a tantrum or becoming irrationally upset, akin to a baby spitting out its pacifier in a fit of anger.

Example: Frustrated by the delay in the schedule, the manager spit the dummy during the team meeting, his outburst surprising the staff who were used to his usual composure.

She'll Be Right

Definition: "She'll be right" is an expression of reassurance commonly used in Australia, implying that everything will turn out okay or fine. It reflects a typically Australian attitude of optimism and resilience in the face of problems.

Example: Despite the setback of their car breaking down, he reassured her with a smile, "She'll be right," confident they could manage the situation and continue their journey.

Stoked

Definition: "Stoked" means being extremely pleased or excited. While not exclusive to Australia, it is commonly used to express high levels of enthusiasm and happiness about an event or achievement.

Example: She was stoked to receive the acceptance letter from her first-choice university, her joy and excitement overflowing as she shared the news with her family.

Struth

Definition: "Struth" is an exclamation of surprise or amazement. This quintessentially Australian expression captures a reaction to astonishing or unbelievable events or information.

Example: "Struth! Can you believe he won the lottery?" he exclaimed, his voice echoing his shock at his friend's sudden windfall.

Spin a Yarn

Definition: "Spin a yarn" means to tell a story, often one that is exaggerated or fabricated. In Australia, this phrase is typically used to describe telling an entertaining but not entirely true tale, often in a light-hearted or humorous context.

Example: Around the campfire, he began to spin a yarn about an exaggerated adventure that had everyone laughing and questioning the reality of his tale.

Sleep with the Fishes

Definition: "Sleep with the fishes" implies being dead, often used in the context of gangster or crime movies. Though not unique to Australia, it's used to suggest that someone has been killed, typically in a grim or mafia-related context.

Example: "If he's not careful with his dealings, he'll end up sleeping with the fishes," the character in the film NOIR warned, hinting at the dangerous consequences of crossing the wrong people.

Stuffed

Definition: In Australia, "stuffed" can mean being very tired, exhausted, or in trouble; it can also refer to having eaten too much. It's a versatile term used to describe various states of discomfort or satiety.

Example: "I'm absolutely stuffed after that huge dinner," she groaned, pushing her plate away, while in another situation, someone might say, "I'm stuffed now—my car won't start, and I'm late for the meeting!"

Sink a Few

Definition: "Sink a few" refers to drinking, especially a few alcoholic beverages. In Australian vernacular, it is a common way to describe enjoying a few drinks in a social setting.

Example: "Let's go down to the pub and sink a few," he suggested after work, inviting his colleagues for some relaxation and camaraderie over beers.

Short End of the Stick

Definition: Getting the "short end of the stick" means receiving a bad deal or the worst part of an agreement. In Australia, this idiom is used to signify receiving less than one deserves, or being at a disadvantage.

Example: She felt she got the short end of the stick when they divided the responsibilities at work, ending up with the most challenging tasks without any additional resources or support.

T

Throw a Shrimp on the Barbie

Definition: "Throw a shrimp on the barbie" is a phrase popularized by an Australian tourism campaign. Despite Australians typically saying "prawn," the phrase suggests grilling and is linked to Australian hospitality and the outdoor lifestyle.

Example: Although he knew Australians said "prawn," he couldn't resist saying "Let's throw a shrimp on the barbie" to his overseas friends, playing up the iconic line they all recognized.

True Blue

Definition: True blue means genuine or authentic, often used to describe something or someone quintessentially Australian.
Example: He's a true blue Aussie, known for his love of cricket, meat pies, and loyalty to mates.

Trackies

Definition: Trackies are tracksuit pants or sweatpants, favoured for their comfort and casual style.
Example: On a lazy Sunday, she lounged around in her trackies, enjoying the relaxed and comfy attire.

Tightarse

Definition: Tightarse is a slang term for someone who is stingy or frugal, often reluctant to spend money.
Example: He's known as a bit of a tightarse, always looking for ways to avoid paying his fair share at group events.

Thingo

Definition: Thingo is an informal term used when the actual name of an object or thing is temporarily forgotten or deemed unimportant.
Example: "Can you pass me that thingo over there?" he asked, pointing to the tool he needed but couldn't recall the name of.

Thongs

Definition: Thongs in Australia refer to flip-flops or sandals, a common footwear choice in the country's warm climate.

Example: Walking along the beach, most people wore thongs, the simple footwear perfect for the sand and surf.

Throw Your Hat in the Ring

Definition: To "throw your hat in the ring" means to show willingness to participate in a contest or take up a challenge. In Australia, this idiom is used to express volunteering or indicating a desire to be part of an activity or competition.

Example: When the company announced the opening for a new project leader, she decided to throw her hat in the ring, ready to take on the challenge and demonstrate her leadership skills.

Throttle

Definition: To throttle means to speed up or accelerate, especially in the context of driving or operating machinery.

Example: Feeling the open road, he throttled the engine, the motorcycle roaring to life as they sped along the highway.

Top End

Definition: The top end refers to the northern regions of Australia, particularly the Northern Territory, known for its tropical climate and unique landscapes.

Example: Visiting the top end, they marvelled at the stunning national parks, rich Indigenous culture, and diverse wildlife.

Tucker

Definition: Tucker is an informal term for food in Australian slang.
Example: After a long day's work, he was looking forward to a good feed of tucker at the local pub.

Tuckerbox

Definition: A tuckerbox is a food container or lunchbox, used to carry meals, especially in a rural or outdoor setting.
Example: He packed his tuckerbox with sandwiches, fruit, and a thermos of tea, ready for a day's work on the farm.

Tart

Definition: "Tart" is a derogatory term used to describe a woman perceived as promiscuous or sexually provocative. It often carries negative judgments and moral implications, reflecting outdated and sexist attitudes.
Example: It's important to recognize that the term "tart" can be offensive and misogynistic, as it perpetuates harmful stereotypes about women's sexual behaviour.

Top Bloke

Definition: "Top bloke" is an Australian term of approval for a man who is well-liked and respected.
Example: Everyone agrees he's a top bloke, always ready to lend a hand and with a kind word for everyone.

Tinny

Definition: Tinny can mean either a can of beer or a small aluminium boat, depending on the context.

Example: They loaded the tinny with fishing gear and a few tinnies for a day out on the river, enjoying both the quiet of the water and the casual beers.

Too Right

Definition: "Too right" is an Australian expression used to strongly agree with someone or to affirm that something is correct.

Example: "This is the best steak I've had in ages," he commented, to which his friend replied, "Too right! It's perfectly cooked."

Taking the Piss

Definition: "Taking the piss" means mocking or making fun of someone or something in a light-hearted way. In Australia, it describes a form of teasing or humorous banter.

Example: When he showed up in a flamboyant outfit, his mates started taking the piss, joking about him being ready for the catwalk rather than the pub.

Take the Mickey

Definition: "Take the mickey" means to tease or mock someone, often in a playful manner. In Australian slang, it's used to describe light-hearted ridicule or banter.

Example: They always take the mickey out of him for his early bedtime, but he takes it in good humour, knowing it's all in fun.

The Full Monty

Definition: "The full monty" means the whole thing or the entire amount, often used to describe complete nudity or having everything included.

Example: For his final performance, he promised it would be the full monty, planning to leave nothing out and give everything he had.

Tell Him He's Dreaming

Definition: "Tell him he's dreaming" is used to indicate that someone's expectations or demands are unrealistic. This phrase became famous through the Australian film "The Castle."

Example: He asked $500 for his old, rusty bike, and they all laughed, one whispering to another, "Tell him he's dreaming!"

Tradie

Definition: A tradie is a tradesperson, such as a carpenter, plumber, or electrician, often working in manual trades or labour.

Example: The tradie arrived early to fix the leaking tap, his expertise and practical skills quickly resolving the issue.

Through Thick and Thin

Definition: "Through thick and thin" means in good times and bad times, denoting loyalty or steadfastness regardless of the circumstances.

Example: They had been friends through thick and thin, supporting each other during both the joys and the trials of life.

Ticker

Definition: In Australian slang, "ticker" refers to the heart, often used metaphorically to talk about one's courage or spirit.

Example: You've got to admire his ticker; despite the setbacks, he keeps pushing forward with such enthusiasm.

U

Ugg Boots/ Uggies

Definition: Ugg boots are sheepskin boots that are worn as casual footwear, known for their warmth and comfort.

Example: In winter, many Australians wear ugg boots to keep their feet warm, the soft sheepskin providing cozy insulation.

Ute

Definition: A ute (short for utility vehicle) is a vehicle with a flatbed or open rear cargo area, often used for carrying goods or equipment.

Example: He loaded the ute with tools and supplies for the job, the vehicle perfectly suited for transporting heavy or bulky items.

Up Yourself

Definition: "Up oneself" means to be arrogant or conceited, implying a high opinion of oneself that others may find annoying or off-putting.

Example: After getting the promotion, he became a bit up himself, flaunting his success without humility.

Uni

Definition: Uni is an informal term for university, commonly used in conversation and writing.

Example: "I'm starting at uni next month," she shared, excited about beginning her higher education journey.

Up and at 'Em

Definition: "Up and at 'em" is an encouragement to get moving or start working on something energetically.

Example: "Come on, up and at 'em! We've got a big day ahead and lots to accomplish," she cheered, rallying her team early in the morning.

Under the Weather

Definition: "Under the weather" means feeling unwell or sick, not in one's usual state of health.

Example: "I'm a bit under the weather today," he explained, struggling with a cold that made him feel lethargic and sniffly.

Unit

Definition: A unit is an informal term for an apartment or flat, a living space that is part of a larger building.

Example: She recently moved into a new unit, enjoying the convenience and simplicity of apartment living.

Up in the Air

Definition: "Up in the air" means something is uncertain or unresolved.

Example: The decision about relocating the company's headquarters is still up in the air, leaving employees anxious about their future at the firm.

Up to Scratch

Definition: "Up to scratch" means meeting a required standard or quality, being satisfactory or adequate.

Example: The manager reviewed the project to ensure everything was up to scratch, meeting the high standards expected by the clients.

Until the Cows Come Home

Definition: "Until the cows come home" is a phrase used to indicate something could continue for a very long time, indefinitely.

Example: They could argue about football until the cows come home, each staunchly defending their favourite team without any sign of agreement.

Under Wraps

Definition: Keeping something "under wraps" means it is kept secret or concealed from public knowledge.

Example: The details of the new product launch are being kept under wraps until the big reveal at the annual conference.

Up and About

Definition: "Up and about" refers to someone being active and moving around, especially after an illness or a rest period.

Example: After a week in bed with the flu, she was finally up and about again, able to join her family for dinner and share in the day's activities.

Up to No Good

Definition: "Up to no good" implies engaging in mischief or dubious activities.

Example: The group of teenagers loitering by the store seemed to be up to no good, casting suspicious glances around and whispering among themselves.

Under the Pump

Definition: Being "under the pump" means experiencing a significant amount of pressure or stress.

Example: With the end-of-year report due tomorrow, she was seriously under the pump, working late into the night to ensure everything was perfect.

Up to the Mark

Definition: "Up to the mark" means meeting the required standard or fulfilling expectations.

Example: His presentation was up to the mark, impressing the clients with its thoroughness and clarity, thereby securing the deal for his company.

V

Vegemite

Definition: Vegemite is a popular Australian spread made from yeast extract, known for its strong, salty flavour, and is a staple in many Australian households.

Example: Every morning, he spread Vegemite on his toast, enjoying the uniquely Australian taste that he grew up with.

Vee Dub

Definition: Vee dub is slang for Volkswagen, a popular car brand known for models like the Beetle and the Golf.

Example: She always dreamed of owning a Vee dub, picturing herself cruising in a vintage VW van along the coast.

Veggie

Definition: Veggie is an informal term for vegetables, commonly used in everyday conversation.

Example: For dinner, they decided to make a colourful veggie stir-fry, packed with fresh produce from the local market.

VB

Definition: VB stands for Victoria Bitter, a well-known brand of beer in Australia, favoured for its distinct flavour.

Example: At the barbecue, the cooler was stocked with cans of VB, a popular choice among the guests.

Vino

Definition: Vino is an informal term for wine, used casually among friends and in social settings.

Example: "Let's open a bottle of vino to celebrate," she suggested, marking the occasion with a favourite wine.

Vibes

Definition: Vibes refer to the atmosphere, feelings, or general mood of a place or situation, often used to describe a positive or negative energy.

Example: The cafe had great vibes, with cosy decor, friendly staff, and a warm, welcoming ambience.

Vote with Your Feet

Definition: "Vote with your feet" means to express an opinion or preference through one's actions, particularly by choosing to leave or attend a place. This idiom is used in Australia to describe how people show their dissatisfaction or support by physically moving to or away from something.

Example: Dissatisfied with the management at her old job, she decided to vote with her feet, joining a competitor that valued employee input and wellbeing.

W

Waltzing Matilda

Definition: "Waltzing Matilda" refers to roaming or traveling with one's belongings, from the famous Australian song, symbolizing a carefree, nomadic lifestyle.

Example: After quitting his job, he went Waltzing Matilda around the country, exploring different towns. The phrase, from Australian slang, means traveling on foot with a "matilda" (swag) slung over one's back and is considered the country's "unofficial national anthem."

Whinge

Definition: To whinge means to complain or whine persistently, often about minor issues or inconveniences.

Example: He had a tendency to whinge about the weather, never quite satisfied whether it was too hot or too cold.

Wowser

Definition: A wowser is a person who is puritanical or opposed to pleasure, often criticising or discouraging activities they consider immoral or improper.

Example: The local wowser campaigned against the new bar, claiming it would lead to moral decay in the community.

Woolies

Definition: Woolies is a colloquial term for Woolworths, one of the major supermarket chains in Australia. Similar to Ameican's Wholefoods or Walart.

Example: "I'm just popping down to Woolies to grab some milk," she mentioned, referring to her quick trip to the supermarket.

Wombat

Definition: A wombat is a burrowing marsupial native to Australia, known for its short legs, strong build, and tendency to dig extensive tunnel systems.

Example: During their camping trip, they spotted a wombat near the site, the creature ambling along before disappearing into its burrow.

Woop Woop

Definition: Woop Woop is an informal term for a remote or isolated place, often used humorously to describe somewhere far away from civilisation.

Example: "He lives out in Woop Woop," they said, indicating that his home was in the middle of nowhere.

Wag

Definition: To wag means to skip or avoid responsibilities, especially used in the context of skipping school or work.

Example: Rather than facing the test, he decided to wag school and spend the day at the arcade.

Wet as a Shag on a Rock

Definition: "Wet as a shag on a rock" means completely soaked or drenched, often used humorously to describe someone or something that is extremely wet.

Example: Caught in the downpour, he arrived home wet as a shag on a rock, water dripping from his clothes and hair.

Wog

Definition: Wog is an informal term for a mild illness or feeling unwell, though it's worth noting the term can be offensive in other contexts.

Example: "I've got a bit of a wog, nothing serious," he explained, feeling under the weather with a cold.

Win Hands Down

Definition: "Win hands down" means to win easily or decisively. In Australia, winning "hands down" implies achieving victory with little to no effort or opposition.

Example: Their team was so well-prepared that they won the debate hands down, with the judges praising their clear arguments and teamwork.

Whopper

Definition: A whopper refers to something very large or impressive, often used to describe an exaggerated story or a large item.

Example: He caught a whopper of a fish on the weekend, the size of the catch becoming the talk of the town.

Wacko

Definition: Wacko means crazy or eccentric, used to describe someone or something that is unusual or outlandish.

Example: The inventor was considered wacko for his bizarre creations, but his genius was undeniable when they became successful.

Wrecked

Definition: Wrecked means very tired or exhausted, often used after a strenuous activity or long day.

Example: After the marathon, she was absolutely wrecked, her body aching but her spirit elated by the achievement.

Wobbly

Definition: A wobbly is a tantrum or outburst, particularly one that is unreasonable or overemotional.

Example: The toddler threw a wobbly in the store, frustrated that he couldn't have the toy he wanted.

Wuss

Definition: Wuss refers to someone who is perceived as weak, cowardly, or easily scared.

Example: They teased him for being a wuss when he refused to watch the horror movie, preferring something less frightening.

Whipper Snipper

Definition: A whipper snipper, also known as a string trimmer or weed eater, is a gardening tool used for trimming grass and weeds.

Example: He used the whipper snipper to tidy up the edges of the lawn, the device efficiently cutting through the overgrown grass.

Wet Blanket

Definition: A "wet blanket" refers to a person who dampens or ruins the fun and enjoyment of others. In Australian usage, it describes someone who is overly pessimistic or spoils the mood by being downbeat or negative.

Example: Just when the party was getting started, he complained about the noise, proving to be a real wet blanket and bringing down everyone's spirits.

Walkabout

Definition: Originally derived from Aboriginal culture, "walkabout" refers to a journey or period of wandering, often spiritual in nature. In a broader Australian context, it means going on a trip or adventure, sometimes spontaneously.

Example: Feeling the need to clear his mind, he went on a walkabout in the Outback, spending time alone in nature to reconnect with himself.

Wide Off the Mark

Definition: "Wide off the mark" means far from being accurate or correct. In Australia, this phrase is used to indicate that an attempt, guess, or judgment is completely wrong or inaccurate.

Example: His predictions about the election results were wide off the mark, as the actual outcomes were drastically different from what he had anticipated.

Warts and All

Definition: "Warts and all" means including all faults or unpleasant aspects. This phrase is used in Australia to suggest accepting or showing something in its true form, without omitting any negative parts.

Example: She decided to write her autobiography warts and all, refusing to leave out any of the less flattering details of her past.

White Knuckle

Definition: "White knuckle" describes experiencing extreme fear or anxiety, often leading to a tense or nervous state. In Australian English, it refers to intense emotions that make someone feel as if they are gripping something tightly in fear.

Example: The turbulent flight caused several passengers to have a white-knuckle experience, holding on tightly to their armrests until the plane landed safely.

Work a Treat

Definition: "Work a treat" means to function exceptionally well or be very effective. In Australian slang, if something "works a treat," it performs better than expected or delivers excellent results.

Example: Adding that new ingredient to the recipe worked a treat, enhancing the flavours and making the dish a huge hit at the dinner party.

<u>Y</u>

Yum Cha

Definition: Yum cha is a type of Chinese dining experience involving tea and a variety of dim sum dishes, popular in many parts of the world, including Australia.

Example: They decided to go for yum cha on Sunday, enjoying the leisurely meal of small dishes and endless cups of tea.

Yonks

Definition: Yonks means a long time, used to indicate that a significant period has passed since an event occurred.
Example: "I haven't seen her in yonks," he remarked, realising how many years had elapsed since they last met.

Yabby

Definition: A yabby is a freshwater crayfish native to Australia, often found in rivers and lakes and used as bait or a food source.
Example: They spent the afternoon yabbying in the creek, hoping to catch enough for a small feast.

Yarn

Definition: Yarn is an informal term for a story or conversation, often one that is entertaining, exaggerated, or lengthy.
Example: He spun a great yarn about his travels, captivating everyone with his tales of adventure and misadventure.

Yesteryear

Definition: "Yesteryear" refers to a time in the past, often evoked nostalgically. In Australian English, it brings to mind an era gone by, usually regarded with fondness or sentimentality.
Example: The exhibition of vintage cars brought back memories of yesteryear, when those models were the height of fashion and innovation.

Yakka

Definition: Yakka is an informal term for work or labour, often implying hard physical effort or strenuous activity.

Example: The construction project required plenty of yakka, with the team putting in long hours to meet the deadline.

Youse

Definition: Youse is an informal, nonstandard plural form of "you," used in some dialects of English, including Australian English.

Example: "Are youse all coming to the BBQ this arvo?" asked the host, using the colloquial term to address the group.

Yowie

Definition: Yowie is a mythical Australian creature akin to Bigfoot or Sasquatch, reputed to live in the wilderness and often featured in folklore and stories.

Example: Campfire tales of the yowie thrilled the children, their imaginations alight with visions of the mysterious bush creature.

You Beauty

Definition: "You beauty" is an exclamation of joy or approval used in Australia to express excitement or happiness about a situation or outcome. It reflects genuine delight or satisfaction in response to something favourable.

Example: When he found out he had won the ticket lottery for the concert, he exclaimed, "You beauty!" thrilled at the unexpected chance to see his favourite band live.

Yeah-Nah

Definition: "Yeah-nah" is a uniquely Australian expression used to say no or express indecision. It begins with an affirmative but is quickly followed by a negative, reflecting ambivalence or a polite way to decline.

Example: "Do you think you'll go back to the same restaurant?" "Yeah-nah, it was good, but I want to try somewhere new."

You Bet

Definition: "You bet" is used in Australia to affirm something with certainty or definiteness. It's a way to strongly agree with someone or confirm a statement enthusiastically.

Example: "Are you coming to the barbecue this weekend?" "You bet! I wouldn't miss it for the world," she replied, excited about the gathering.

Yonder

Definition: "Yonder" refers to a place that is some distance in the direction indicated; over there. Although not exclusively Australian, it's used in rural and colloquial Australian English to refer to a location that is visible but not immediately nearby.

Example: "Where's the farm you were talking about?" "Just over yonder, past the creek. You can see the barn from here."

You Little Ripper

Definition: "You little ripper" is an exclamation of delight or enthusiasm, similar to "you beauty." It's used in Australia to celebrate success or express excitement about good news.

Example: When he nailed the presentation and secured the client, his colleague cheered, "You little ripper!" proud and thrilled by his success.

You Don't Say

Definition: "You don't say" is a sarcastic remark used in Australia to express that something is obvious or well-known, often feigning surprise.

Example: "Did you know it gets really hot here in the summer?" "You don't say," she replied dryly, as the sun blazed on yet another scorching day.

Z

Zebra Crossing

Definition: A "zebra crossing" is a type of pedestrian crossing marked with alternating white and dark stripes on the road, resembling a zebra's pattern. In Australia, it specifically refers to these crossings designed to enhance pedestrian safety.

Example: He waited at the zebra crossing, watching as cars stopped to let him cross the street safely from one side to the other.

Zilch

Definition: Zilch means nothing or zero, used to emphasize the complete absence of something.

Example: Despite all the hype, there was zilch evidence to support the outrageous claims made by the product's promoters.

Zinc

Definition: Zinc is an informal term for sunscreen, especially the thick, visible kind used for high sun protection.

Example: Before hitting the beach, they slathered on the zinc to protect their skin from the harsh sun.

Zest

Definition: Zest represents enthusiasm or energy, showing a keen interest or eagerness in doing something.

Example: He tackled the project with zest, his passion and dedication evident in his proactive approach.

Zingy

Definition: Zingy describes something lively, energetic, or having a sharp taste or flavor, often used to describe food or personalities.

Example: The salad dressing was zingy, with a tangy lemon flavor that refreshed the palate.

Zoo

Definition: Zoo, used metaphorically, refers to a chaotic or disorderly situation where things are out of control.

Example: With everyone talking at once and kids running around, the meeting turned into a complete zoo.

Zipped

Definition: Zipped means to move quickly or hastily, often with speed and efficiency.

Example: He zipped past me on his bike, barely slowing down as he navigated through the park.

Zoomer

Definition: Zoomer refers to someone or something that moves fast or is energetic, often used to describe a dynamic and active person.

Example: The young athlete was a real zoomer on the track, outrunning competitors with her impressive speed.

Zillion

Definition: Zillion is a hyperbolic term for an extremely large number or amount, used to emphasize vastness or exaggeration.

Example: He seemed to have a zillion ideas for the project, each one more creative and ambitious than the last.

Zero in on

Definition: "Zero in on" means to focus closely or concentrate on something. It's used to describe directing one's attention or efforts toward a specific goal, object, or task.

Example: As the deadline approached, she had to zero in on the most critical aspects of the project to ensure it met all the necessary requirements.

Zip it

Definition: "Zip it" is a command to stop talking or be quiet. It's a colloquial way to tell someone to cease speaking, often used in a playful or firm manner depending on the context.

Example: "If you can't keep from spoiling the movie, you'll just have to zip it," he said half-jokingly to his friend who was notorious for revealing plot twists.

Zooper Dooper

Definition: "Zooper Dooper" refers to a brand of popular flavoured ice blocks in Australia. These ice treats are a staple during the hot summer months, fondly remembered by adults and beloved by children for their variety of flavours.

Example: At the family barbecue, the children were treated to Zooper Doopers, their faces lighting up as they chose from the rainbow of flavours, a perfect respite from the summer heat.

Zonked

Definition: Zonked means being extremely tired or exhausted, often to the point of needing immediate rest.

Example: After the marathon, he was completely zonked and fell asleep as soon as he hit the couch.

Zero Tolerance

Definition: "Zero tolerance" refers to a policy of strict enforcement without any exceptions. In the Australian context, it indicates a firm, uncompromising approach to regulating certain behaviours, particularly in environments like schools or public spaces.

Example: The school adopted a zero tolerance policy towards bullying, making it clear that such behaviour would lead to immediate and significant consequences to ensure a safe environment for all students.

Made in the USA
Columbia, SC
22 December 2024

50452952R00096